# Edinburgh Review 139

## *Now Would Be The Right Time*

Edinburgh Review
Editor: Alan Gillis
Assistant editor and production: Jennie Renton
Marketing and events: Lynsey May

Advisory Board: Janice Galloway, Kathleen Jamie, Robert Alan Jamieson, James Loxley, Brian McCabe, Randall Stevenson, Alan Warner

Published by Edinburgh Review, 22a Buccleuch Place, Edinburgh EH8 9LN
edinburghreview@ed.ac.uk
www.edinburgh-review.com

Individual subscriptions (3 issues annually) £20 within the UK; £28 abroad. Institutional subscriptions (3 issues annually) £35 within the UK; £43 abroad. Most back issues are available at £7.99 each. You can subscribe online at www.edinburgh-review.com or send a cheque to Edinburgh Review, 22a Buccleuch Place, Edinburgh EH8 9LN

Edinburgh Review 139
*Now Would Be The Right Time*

ISBN 978-0-9928378-0-8
ISSN 0267-6672

© the contributors 2014
Printed and bound in the UK
by Bell & Bain Ltd, Glasgow

*Edinburgh Review*
is supported by

# Contents

## Poetry

| | |
|---|---|
| Peter McDonald | 29 |
| Ciaran Carson | 46 |
| Jane McKie | 64 |
| David Harsent | 78 |
| Miriam Gamble | 91 |
| Ricardo Pau-Llosa | 107 |
| Colette Bryce | 122 |
| Rody Gorman | 133 |

## Fiction

| | |
|---|---|
| Dilys Rose | 41 |
| Brian Hamill | 71 |
| Regi Claire | 98 |
| Daniel Shand | 126 |

## Articles

| | |
|---|---|
| Dennis O'Driscoll | 7 |
| David Wheatley | 54 |
| Fran Brearton | 82 |
| Colin Graham | 111 |

## Reviews

| | |
|---|---|
| W.N. Herbert on Dorn | 139 |
| Simon Malpas on Pynchon | 145 |

| | |
|---|---|
| Maria Johnston on Kleinzahler | 148 |
| Ben Wilkinson on Laird | 153 |
| Allyson Stack on Saunders | 156 |
| Simon Pomery on Boast | 159 |
| Paul Maddern on Berry | 161 |
| Aingeal Clare on Mahon | 165 |
| Martin Philip on Hendry | 168 |
| Rody Gorman on Crichton Smith translations | 171 |
| | |
| Notes on Contributors | 173 |
| Subscription Information | 176 |

In memory of Seamus Heaney and Dennis O'Driscoll

*Dennis O'Driscoll*

# Lux Perpetua:
## *Seamus Heaney's* Electric Light

In Seamus Heaney's collections the last shall usually be first. Many critics over the years have observed that the final poem in a Heaney volume will serve advance notice of what may be expected in the collection that follows. Blake Morrison, who – in his 1982 study of the poet – pioneered this prognostic or divinatory approach to the Heaney canon, wrote of *Field Work* (1979) that it begins 'not at the beginning but, as is Heaney's custom, with the last poem of the book that preceded it'. The critic is not reproving the poet for repetition but admiring Heaney's orderly transfer of power from book to succeeding book, as – in Morrison's own words – he 'takes up and develops' the theme of the final poem of the previous collection. *Field Work* – in which the Ulster-born Heaney puts down roots in the Irish Republic – continues to probe artistic and political dilemmas of the kind adumbrated in 'Exposure', the closing poem of *North* (1975). In time, the 'Ugolino' episode from Dante's *Inferno*, with which *Field Work* ended, would point the way forward to the penitential *purgatorio* of the title sequence of *Station Island* (1984); and the 'bare wire' poetry plaited into the 'Sweeney Redivivus' sequence, the third and final section of *Station Island*, would lead towards the plain-speaking parables of *The Haw Lantern* (1987). 'And so on', as Heaney himself writes in the final line of 'The Thimble' in *The Spirit Level* (1996).

'The Thimble' was not the last word in *The Spirit Level*. The collection ended with one of Heaney's most affecting poems, 'Postscript', retracing a wind-buffeted drive on Ireland's west coast; a drive in which the light and the foam and the sight of 'a flock of swans' (maybe even a Yeatsian 'nine-and-fifty' of the birds) left him inwardly as well as outwardly shaken:

> Useless to think you'll park and capture it
> More thoroughly. You are neither here nor there,
> A hurry through which known and strange things pass
> As big soft buffetings come at the car sideways
> And catch the heart off guard and blow it open.

As early as 1979, when he turned forty, Seamus Heaney was expressing concern that, as one gets older, the 'space occupied by the instinctual life' contracts. Nearly twenty years later 'Postscript' rejoices not only in the vision of the slate-grey lake and foaming ocean, swans and sky, which he has been momentarily granted but also in the tenacity of inspiration, the capacity of an ageing heart to still spontaneously respond to the world, to be caught 'off guard' and, in an image used irenically and almost ironically by an Ulster poet, blown open. 'Postscript' is such a risky poem, so tentative, so contingent, that it would be difficult to retrospectively press it into service as offering any tangible clues about Heaney's ensuing collection, *Electric Light* (published five years after *The Spirit Level*), except in the general sense of affirming the poet's determination to keep his imaginative arteries open for the next hoped-for flush of inspiration, the next heartfelt epiphany.

Even if 'Postscript' fails to fully conform to the soothsaying theory of Heaney's work, it does find an exact companion piece in the poem, 'Ballynahinch Lake', included in *Electric Light*. Beginning briskly with 'so', the much-discussed opening word of Heaney's *Beowulf* translation, a word strongly suggestive of an ongoing narrative, the poem is a postscript to 'Postscript'. The setting again is a lake with 'waterbirds' in western Ireland, but it is no longer 'useless to think you'll park and capture' the scene: 'this time, yes, it had indeed / Been useful to stop'. If the swan-bearing lake of 'Postscript' has its literary antecedent in 'The Wild Swans at Coole', 'Ballynahinch Lake' may owe something to Wordsworth's 'uncertain heaven received / Into the bosom of the steady lake'. In neither 'Postscript' nor 'Ballynahinch Lake', however, does Heaney's respect for his literary elders stifle his own voice; pace, language and imagery all conspire to reveal his authorship:

> So we stopped and parked in the spring-cleaning light
> Of Connemara on a Sunday morning
> As a captivating brightness held and opened

> And the utter mountain mirrored in the lake
> Entered us like a wedge knocked sweetly home
> Into core timber.

Heaney's acknowledgement of his literary peers and forebears, principally confined to his essays and interviews at first, has increasingly spilled over into his poems through citation, homage, dedication and elegy. If Yeats and Wordsworth are subtly present in the poems just mentioned, so representative a cross-section of the literary and mythological pantheon – including Virgil, Graves, Brodsky, Hopkins, Kavanagh and any number of figures from Greek literature and mythology – populates *Electric Light* that Heaney may seem in danger of reaching reflexively for a literary quotation or developing an over-dependency on poetical or mythological allusions. While such dangers are real, it is bracing to behold a poet – especially one whose vast readership extends far beyond the academy – refusing to pander to lazy populism and, instead, choosing to make ever-greater intellectual demands on his audience without losing contact with his 'instinctual life'.

The Latin fragments, Greek and Irish myths, Shakespearean quotations and *Beowulf* references will perplex admirers of Heaney's early books where an occasional cameo appearance by Undine, Venus or Narcissus was the only barrier between the reader and uncomplicated lyrical bliss. Yet Heaney is still capable of eidetic lyrical poetry, as transparent as the 'water-roof' through which he spies on the fish in the single-sentence 'Perch', a one-movement masterpiece of water music:

> Perch on their water-perch hung in the clear Bann River
> Near the clay bank in alder-dapple and waver,
>
> Perch we called 'grunts', little flood-slubs, runty and ready,
> I saw and I see in the river's glorified body
>
> That is passable through, but they're bluntly holding the pass,
> Under the water-roof, over the bottom, adoze,
>
> Guzzling the current, against it, all muscle and slur
> In the finland of perch, the fenland of alder, on air

> That is water, on carpets of Bann stream, on hold
> In the everything flows and steady go of the world.

The reader of 'Perch', with its fluid syntax and liquid rhythms, its assonance and echo, its gestures towards end-rhymes, its visual puns and vivid use of dialect words, is likely to be swept along with the flow of this apparently simple poem before noting that it, too, contains numerous allusions – to the Bible, Heraclitus and Hopkins's 'Pied Beauty', for example. And yet readers who do not respond to these stimuli will nonetheless be rewarded with a verbally, musically and imagistically satisfying poem; as with the River Bann itself, they are offered an option on a wade in the shallows or a dunk in the deeper currents, just as the poet himself always seems adept both at walking on water and sounding its depths. Heaney remains, almost uniquely in contemporary poetry, an erudite poet who educates rather than alienates his non-specialist readers; a poet who is as comfortable with Virgil's *Eclogues* as with a popular song like 'The Rose of Mooncoin', who can effortlessly situate Stanley Kubrick's *2001: A Space Odyssey* and 'Bob Cushley with his jennet' within the compass of a single poem.

Heaney's example is an instructive one for the future of poetry in English. Although his books outsell any other living poet in the language he is steadfast and uncompromising in his standards and – in the face of the challenges of literary theory and literary politics – stoutly defends the literary canon as a thriving, evolving force. His version of *Beowulf*, an Anglo-Saxon heroic narrative which even college students of Early English tended to shun, on grounds of tedium, single-handedly revived the fortunes of that poem for scholars as well as a general readership. In doing so, he gave practical expression to forthright remarks about the canon, written in 1991, which form part of his essay 'On Poetry and Professing':

> Poets are… more likely to attest without self-consciousness to the living nature of poetic tradition and to the demotic life of 'the canon'. Nowadays, undergraduates are being taught prematurely to regard the poetic heritage as an oppressive imposition and to suspect it for its latent discriminations in the realm of gender, its privilegings and marginalisations in the realms of class and power. All of this suspicion may be salutary enough when it is exercised by a mind informed by that which it is being taught to suspect,

but it is a suspicion which is lamentably destructive of cultural memory when it is induced in minds without any cultural possessions whatever. On the other hand, when a poet quotes from memory or from prejudice or in sheer admiration, 'the canon' is manifested in an educationally meaningful way. To put it simply, I believe that the life of society is better served by a quotation-bore who quotes out of a professional love than by an 'unmasking'-bore who subverts out of theory.

Typical of the way in which Heaney educates his audience and avoids confounding a general readership is through subtle illustration or annotation of his more arcane references. Having, in *North*, recollected that 'Archimedes thought he could move the world if he could find the right place to position his lever', his own work has always been positioned so as to move (in every sense) the world to the largest possible extent, whether through the leverage of short slim-fit lyrics or longer, roomier sequences. Increasingly, he has experimented with what he terms 'loose-weave' poems: 'Keeping Going' and 'The Flight Path' in *The Spirit Level*; 'Out of the Bag', 'Known World' and the aptly-titled 'The Loose Box' in *Electric Light*.

'Out of the Bag', for instance, quickly swerves from innocent opening stanzas about the doctor's arrival in the Heaney household, where his mother will again give birth ('All of us came in Doctor Kerlin's bag'), to allusions to the hyperboreans and the sanctuaries of Asclepius. His description of Doctor Kerlin's eyes as 'hyperborean' is immediately glossed with the explanatory 'beyond-the-north-wind' blue. Readers hitherto unfamiliar with the term 'hyperborean' can then discern it for themselves, later in the book, in the opening line of 'To the Shade of Zbigniew Herbert' ('You were one of those from the back of the north wind'), or where Heaney himself, on vacation in Greece, becomes 'hyper, boozed, borean'.

Similarly, in 'Out of the Bag', the uninitiated reader is put at ease when Heaney refers to the sanctuaries of Asclepius. He explains, through consultations with '*poeta doctus* Peter Levi' and '*poeta doctus* [Robert] Graves', that those sanctuaries were 'the equivalent of hospitals / In ancient Greece. Or of shrines like Lourdes'; and he memorably describes his own visits to the site of the temple of Asclepius ('It was midday, mid-May, pre-tourist sunlight') and Lourdes ('Hatless, groggy, shadowing myself') – just as, elsewhere in the collection, places like Arcadia and the Castalian Spring are lifted out of myth and quickened into life when his own spirited adventures in these real and resonant locations are recounted. Indeed, in 'Sonnets from Hellas', a living goatherd chanced upon 'in the forecourt of the filling station' at Arcadia is described as 'subsisting beyond eclogue and translation'. Heaney's exposure to the poetry of Zbigniew Herbert and Miroslav Holub, two East Europeans who frequently drew on ancient Greek literature, will have helped to convince him of the continued prolificacy of classical myths; these poets, whom he championed in *The Government of the Tongue* (1988), proved their classical and mythological allusions to be resilient enough to survive censorship and universal enough to survive translation into English.

In his own practice as a translator – of Old English, Old Irish and classical works – Seamus Heaney has been scrupulously respectful towards the original texts, having learned from his long labour on *Sweeney Astray* (1983) that an 'obedient, literal' approach yielded more substantial dividends than an imitation of the skilful but exploitative asset-stripping in which Robert Lowell engaged in *Imitations*. There is nothing reverentially dull or piously po-faced about Heaney's translations, however, and his ability to resurrect and revitalise an ancient text can be witnessed in miniature in 'Moling's Gloss', one of the brief poems clustered in *Electric Light* under the title 'Ten Glosses' (spontaneous Gaelic poems inscribed in the margins of early monastic manuscripts were termed 'glosses'). This four-line poem, dating from the tenth century and rhyming *a-a-b-b*, is attributed to Moling (presumably the saint with whom the protagonist reaches an 'uneasy reconciliation' in the closing pages of *Sweeney Astray*). In a literal prose rendition by the scholar Gerard Murphy, it reads: 'When I am among my seniors I am proof that games are forbidden; when I am among the wild they think I am younger than they.' Responding gamely to the humour of the Gaelic text and retaining its terse musicality (though altering the rhyme scheme), Heaney's poem replenishes the original with a contemporary colloquial 'gloss':

> Among my elders, I know better
> And frown on any carry-on;
> Among the brat-pack on the batter
> I'm taken for a younger man.

Colloquial, too, is the translation of 'Virgil: Eclogue IX' in *Electric Light* ('watch / The boyo with the horns doesn't go for you') but makes no attempt to enact Virgil in present-day dress. What lends a modern reverberation to this faithfully rendered poem is not so much the register of Heaney's language as Virgil's own political undertones ('An outsider lands and says he has the rights / To our bit of ground') and, above all, the debate – redolent of the quandaries aired in the opening essay of *The Government of the Tongue* – about the efficacy of art in the face of terror ('songs and tunes / Can no more hold out against brute force than doves / When eagles swoop'). In translating 'Eclogue IX' Heaney is again assisting his readers: in this case, by providing, for an age in which classical studies have waned, a context in which his two other poems in eclogue form – neither of them a translation – may be read. In addition, he is enlarging the modern eclogue tradition to which some of the best twentieth-century poets contributed, including Robert Hass, Heaney's fellow Ulsterman Louis MacNeice, and the doomed Hungarian poet Miklós Radnóti. Radnóti began work on his devastating poems after he had translated the same Virgil eclogue as Heaney (IX), having no doubt similarly discovered the potential of the form to serve as a personal and political echo chamber. Heaney himself has tellingly written of Virgil's *Eclogues*: 'What these poems prove is that literariness as such is not an abdication from the truth. The literary is one of the methods human beings have devised for getting at reality…'

'Glanmore Eclogue', a light, playful poem, set in a part of County Wicklow about which Heaney has been writing since *Field Work*, acknowledges the gap between modern poet and wary contemporary reader. A farmer figure, Myles, urges the poet to offer 'words that the rest of us / Can understand'. This eclogue is essentially a fulsome tribute to Ann Saddlemyer, called 'Augusta' in the poem – after Lady Gregory whose plays she edited. Saddlemyer, who owned Glanmore Cottage, is termed (in a Yeatsian epigraph to 'Glanmore Sonnets' which again tacitly acknowledges the parallel with Lady Gregory) the Heaney family's 'heartiest welcomer' to Wicklow; she is best-known as a Synge scholar (the playwright – assigned the Virgilian name, Meliboeus, in this eclogue – had close family ties with Glanmore). 'Glanmore Eclogue' also portrays a Southern Ireland in which the small farmers who regained their 'bit of ground' politically are being 'priced out of the market' economically in the Celtic Tiger conditions that prevailed in the 1990s. Like Virgil, Heaney has a first-hand knowledge of farming; the 'cows in clover' of 'Eclogue IX', with 'canted teats / And tightening udders', are the same breed as the County Derry herd which appears in the richly maternal and indeed mammarial final stanza of 'Bann Valley Eclogue', much the most impressive of the three eclogues in the collection:

> Child on the way, it won't be long until
> You land among us. Your mother's showing signs,
> Out for her sunset walk among big round bales.
> Planet earth like a teething ring suspended
> Hangs by its world-chain. Your pram waits in the corner.
> Cows are let out. They're sluicing the milk-house floor.

The epigraph to 'Bann Valley Eclogue', '*Sicelides Musae, paulo maiora canamus*' ('Sicilian Muses, sing we greater things' in Sir John Beaumont's enduring version), is the first line of Virgil's 'Golden Age' or 'Messianic' eclogue, Number IV. 'Bann Valley Eclogue' is not so much a parallel translation as an independent text, which is aware of – without being dependent on – the trajectory of Virgil's poem. If Heaney yields to hopes of a golden age for the child whose birth is anticipated in his eclogue, it is because she is being born into a post-ceasefire Ulster; and if the poem predicts an auspicious event, it is not the arrival of a male Messiah. Virgil's expectations of a male birth contrast with Heaney's certainty that the young woman in the poem is bearing a daughter; the baby's father is unmentioned and the only identifiable male presence – aside from Virgil – is Heaney himself remembering (through a skein of exhaustively exact adjectives) the shamrock 'with its twining, binding, creepery, tough, thin roots' which he picked for his own mother on St Patrick's Day.

An eclogue can be a miniature drama and Seamus Heaney has long shown an interest in pitching voice against line, metre against speech: in a radio verse-play (*Munro*), versions of Sophocles (*The Cure at Troy, The Burial at Thebes*) and the dramatic monologues in *Station Island*. One of the most enjoyable and entertaining poems in *Electric Light* is 'The Real Names' – a drama in ten brief scenes. The setting: St Columb's College in Derry, c.1954; the dramatis personae: Seamus Heaney and his classmates. Shakespeare, though, is the real hero of the poem: his language has engraved itself deeply into Heaney's memory; and school performances of his dramas (in which – true to Elizabethan practice – female parts were played by boys) are fondly and humorously recollected. As an Irish poet from the nationalist tradition,

Heaney has no wish to speak the Queen's English ('My passport's green. / No glass of ours was ever raised / To toast *The Queen*'); but he is proud to speak Shakespeare's tongue. It takes only the merest whisper from the inner prompter – the name of a character from *The Tempest*, a line or two from *The Merchant of Venice*, an image from *Henry IV Part I* – to transport him to that oak-beamed corner of his memory where a chain of Shakespearean associations is set in motion.

The most virtuosic cadenza in the poem is an offshoot of a line from *Hamlet*:

> There is a willow grows aslant the brook
> But in the beginning it was sally tree.
> Sallies in hedges and sallies on the bank
> Of the Moyola River and black sallies
> Like a line of daunted stragglers bogging down
> In the sedge and glarry wetness of our meadow.
> The one in the yard was tetter-barked and hollow,
> Two-timing earth and air: corona top
> Of flick-and-shimmer, sprout-and-tremble growth…

One of Seamus Heaney's favourite poems by Robert Lowell, 'Epilogue', pleads for 'each figure in the photograph' to be accorded 'his living name'. 'The Real Names' not only reveals the identities of those who participated with Heaney in school productions but also lays considerable stress on local habitations and local names – in this instance, Hamlet's willow at Elsinore is supplanted by Heaney's sally at the Moyola River in County Derry. 'Sally' is a regional variant on sallow (from the Latin, *salix*, for willow). One is reminded of Heaney's 'Mossbawn' essay, in which he remarks of Keats's 'Ode to Autumn': 'I had a vague satisfaction from "the small gnats mourn / Among the river sallows", which would have been complete if it had been "midges" mourning among the "sallies".'

This localising tendency – already seen in the substitution of Heaney's Glanmore and Bann Valley for Virgil's Arcadia – resurfaces in 'On His Work in the English Tongue', a poem in celebration and commemoration of Ted Hughes. As an elegy for a close friend (albeit a fellow writer), this is an intensely literary poem. Even here, however, in the surge of a breathtakingly bravura description of the underside of a bridge ('the tremor-drip / And cranial acoustic of the stone'), Heaney specifies that the structure – which the reader might otherwise have assumed to be a generic bridge or perhaps a bridge in Ted Hughes's Yorkshire – is in fact 'the one / Over the railway lines at Anahorish' in County Derry.

Seamus Deane has termed Heaney's insistence on the local a species of 'domestication... a search for an origin'. No wonder Heaney has quoted Carson McCullers to the effect that 'to know who you are, you have to have a place to come from' and has cited Patrick Kavanagh as illustrative of the fact that 'Loved places are important places, and the right names "snatch out of time the passionate transitory".' Exotic ground on the road to Piedras Blancas in Spain is compared with the 'home ground, / The Gaeltacht, say, in the nineteen-fifties'. 'The Gaeltacht' (the title refers to one of the Irish-speaking districts of Ireland), a yearning poem comprising a roll-call of friends from student days, is Heaney's 'imitation' of Dante's sonnet to Guido Cavalcanti. And the Irish language is again a 'domesticating' medium in 'Desfina' (one of the 'Sonnets from Hellas') where numerous and humorous Irish equivalents for Mount Parnassus spill out over dinner with the ouzo:

> Mount Parnassus placid on the skyline:
> *Slieve na mBard, Knock Filiocht, Ben Duan.*
> We gaelicised new names for Poetry Hill
> As we wolfed down horta, tarama and houmos
> At sunset in the farmyard, drinking ouzos...

'Known World', improvised in form and innovative in theme, demonstrates the importance for Heaney of self-identification when faced with foreign settings. In the poem he draws vivid comparisons between Belgrade in the Balkans and Belmullet in Ireland ('Belmullet elders in the streets. / Black shawls, straight walk, the weather eye, the beads'). It is with the empathetic solidarity of a farmer's son that he writes of the rural people displaced by a Kosovan conflict (the poem is dated May 1998), simultaneously viewing them through the 'cloud-boil of a camera lens' and the lens of memory:

> At the still centre of the cardinal points
> The flypaper hung from our kitchen ceiling,

> Honey-strip and death-trap, a barley-sugar twist
> Of glut and loathing…
>                           In a nineteen-fifties
> Of iron stoves and kin groups still in place,
> Congregations blackening the length
> And breadth of summer roads.
>                           And now the refugees
> Come loaded on tractor mudguards and farm carts,
> On trailers, ruck-shifters, box-barrows, prams,
> On sticks, on crutches, on each other's shoulders…

The allusion to T.S. Eliot's 'Burnt Norton' in those lines is not the only literary reference in 'Known World'. In fact, much of the poem focuses on Heaney's recollections of the companionably bibulous Struga Poetry Festival in Macedonia in 1978 when 'we hardly ever sobered'. Always mindful of the dangers of exploiting the woes of others ('"punting along" on other people's weeping wounds'), he places his images of suffering in the context of his first-hand reminiscences of the Balkan region. Exactly as in *Field Work*, when Ulster violence was at issue ('How culpable was he / That last night when he broke / Our tribe's complicity?'), he prefers to raise pertinent questions than to make presumptuous assertions: 'who's to know / How to read sorrow rightly, or at all?' The vignettes of the Struga Festival recreate the giddy exuberance of the occasion – the banter, the booze, the camaraderie – with a wry immediacy. In fact, some of the memories of people (Hans Magnus Enzensberger in panama hat and 'pressed-to-a-T cream linen suit') and events (including a sensuously sketched Madonna's Day gathering in the mountains) owe their freshness to their origins in contemporaneous notes:

>                  Then, the notebook says,
> 'People on the move, field full of folk,
> Packhorses with panniers, uphill push
> Of families, unending pilgrim stream.
> Today is workers' day in memory
> Of General Strike. Also Greek Orthodox
> Madonna's Day.'

This reliance on raw notes is not a feature unique to 'Known World'.

One of the previous high points of Heaney's work, the final section of 'The Flight Path' in *The Spirit Level,* ends: 'Eleven in the morning. I made a note: / "Rock-lover, loner, sky-sentry, all hail!" / And somewhere the dove rose. And kept on rising.' *Field Work* – written when his entrancement with Robert Lowell was at its height – contains a poem, 'High Summer', in which lines are quoted from a notebook or letter. 'Known World' is significant in the evolution of Seamus Heaney's work for the daring admixture of its registers and the unprecedented heterogeneity of its parts. It is as if the poet were insouciantly exploring a new poetry path, still willing to risk fresh directions and at last admitting into his work, albeit self-deprecatingly, the experiences of the international literary traveller (which, at this post-Nobel juncture, it would be dishonest to exclude).

The international literary life features also – but less centrally – in a poem in memory of Joseph Brodsky, 'Audenesque'. This poem, one of a number of elegies grouped together in the second part of *Electric Light*, is an instance of what Heaney himself has classified as 'the Lycidas syndrome' whereby 'one artist's sense of vocation and purpose is sent into crisis by the untimely death of another'. We are allowed backstage at a reading in Western Massachusetts, where Brodsky is decanting pepper vodka, and are taken on board a train in Finland ('Lenin's train-trip in reverse') where Brodsky and Heaney are 'swapping manuscripts and quips'. Heaney's imitative ingenuity in 'Audenesque' is both formal and linguistic: formal in its borrowings from 'Wystan Auden's metric feet', the trochaic tetrameter employed in the third section of 'In Memory of W.B. Yeats'; linguistic in the way it affectionately and accurately replicates the clumsiness of Brodsky's English verse. In a *New York Times Book Review* tribute to Brodsky, Heaney commented on Brodsky's 'bewilderment at the self-delusion of second raters' in poetry. But for many of us not privileged to have enjoyed the friendship of this courageous and charismatic man, Brodsky's own first-rateness was a matter for conjecture or for trust, as the 'more-than-enoughness' which Heaney associates with true poetry veered towards a kind of 'over-the-topness'. Heaney's mimetic virtuosity captures Brodsky's gauche verbosity:

> Nevermore that wild speed-read,
> Nevermore your tilted head
> Like a deck where mind took off

>     With a mind-flash and a laugh,
>
>     Nevermore that rush to pun
>     Or to hurry through all yon
>     Jammed enjambements piling up
>     As you went above the top,
>
>     Nose in air, foot to the floor,
>     Revving English like a car…

The exceptional aptness of 'In Memory of W.B. Yeats' as a model for an elegy of Joseph Brodsky lies not only in Brodsky's lifelong obsession with Auden, and his devotion to this elegy for Yeats, but also in the fact that both Yeats and Brodsky died on the same 'double-crossed and death-marched date, / January twenty-eight'. It was during his enforced exile (as a so-called 'social parasite') in the Arkhangelsk region of Northern Russia that Brodsky wrote his 'Verses on the Death of T S Eliot', modelled on Auden's elegy.

'"Would They Had Stay'd"', the finest of the literary elegies clustered in the disappointingly uneven second part of *Electric Light*, is a lament for a quartet of recent Scottish poets that takes its title from Shakespeare's 'Scottish play'. In approaching his task Heaney will have been conscious of the majestic precedent set by 'Lament for the Makaris', William Dunbar's elegy which he first encountered as a student and which, having modernised the late medieval Scottish text, he recorded for Harvard University's Poetry Room. The four poets lamented by Heaney are Norman MacCaig, George Mackay Brown, the Gaelic-language Somhairle MacGill-Eain (under his more familiar English name, Sorley MacLean) and the bilingual Iain Crichton Smith (under his less familiar Gaelic Name, Iain MacGabhainn). The poem contains heroic and heraldic language, worthy of a medieval poem, as well as some interlinked images of deer whose presence in the five sections of the poem is the golden thread that binds this elegy together:

>     The colour of meadow hay, with its meadow-sweet
>     And liver-spotted dock leaves, they were there
>     Before we noticed them, all eyes and evening,
>     Up to their necks in the meadow.

Not all of the elegies concern literary figures – the deeply touching

'Seeing the Sick', for example, memorialises the poet's father. Although his father was an unliterary man and (as commemorated in 'The Stone Verdict') a taciturn one, Heaney looks to his own literary forefather, Gerard Manley Hopkins, for an elegiac template with which he can feel comfortable – perhaps because it would have been out of character, embarrassing even, for son to address father directly in matters involving the emotions and affections. Hopkins's elegy for a 'big-boned and hardy-handsome' blacksmith facilitates Heaney's oblique and clipped, but intense and unfeigned, tribute to his cattle-dealing father. The poem's title, its opening phrase ('anointed and all') and much of its imagery derive from Hopkins's 'Felix Randal'; Heaney and Hopkins use the word 'tendered' differently (Hopkins in connection with Holy Communion, Heaney with the more secular balm of morphine) but with an equal upwelling of tendresse. The literary imagery illuminates the human portrait and no more occludes the dying father than the allusions to Chaucer, Shakespeare, Dante and Larkin erase the 'desperate' grandmother in the poem 'Electric Light'. The sybilline grandmother's 'urgent, sibilant / *Ails*' excavates an imaginative channel for the poet into England, the English language and great English literature. Again, Heaney shows himself to be a poet so attuned to every verbal nuance that a single word can detonate the history of an entire language:

> We were both desperate
>
> The night I was left to stay, when I wept and wept
> Under the clothes, under the waste of light
> Left turned on in the bedroom. 'What ails you, child,
>
> What ails you, for God's sake?' Urgent, sibilant
> Ails, far off and old. Scarcesome cavern waters
> Lapping a boatslip. Her helplessness no help.
>
> \*
>
> Lisp and relapse. Eddy of sybilline English.
> Splashes between a ship and dock, to which,
> *Animula*, I would come alive in time
> As ferries churned and turned down Belfast Lough

> Towards the brow-to-glass transport of a morning train,
> The very 'there-you-are-and-where-are-you?'
>
> Of poetry itself. Backs of houses
> Like the back of hers, meat-safes and mangles
> In the railway-facing yards of fleeting England,
>
> An allotment scarecrow among patted rigs,
> Then a town-edge soccer pitch, the groin of distance,
> Fields of grain like the Field of the Cloth of Gold.
>
> To Southwark too I came,
> From tube-mouth into sunlight,
> Moyola-breath by Thames's 'straunge stronde'.

His grandmother's use of 'ails' deepened the child's sense of homesickness because it was at variance with the usage in his own Mossbawn household (where – as the prose-poem, 'Hedge-School' reveals – 'What are you crying about now, son?' would be the family formula) – early evidence of the future poet's ultra-sensitivity to language! The proximity of 'ails' to 'nails' acts as a mnemonic for Heaney whose abiding memory of his grandmother is of her 'smashed thumb-nail'. Perhaps the further proximity of 'nail' to 'alien' is not accidental either, in a poem which opens with his alienation in the strange life and light of his grandmother's house. The electric light there, to which he was unaccustomed at the time, is now transformed into the *lux perpetua* of poetry as the poem comes to rest on an elegiac note 'among beads and vertebrae in the Derry ground'.

Seamus Heaney's words have never been mere ciphers, tools which simply record events and re-order experiences. As a devoted exponent of Eliot's 'auditory imagination', words for Heaney are sounds before they are sense or, rather, their sounds are inextricably linked to their sense. By *Wintering Out* (1972) he had begun making language his subject as well as his medium. Just as people's names are sometimes said to contain their destinies, Heaney's place names contain their topography ('*Anahorish*, soft gradient / of consonant, vowel-meadow'). In *Electric Light* 'ails' is not the only troubling word Heaney has borne with him across the years; as a boarder at St Columb's College, he was 'left… winded' by the ominous power packed into the word 'attack' which he heard in connection with 'The Border Campaign' in Ulster in 1956.

While poets should, by virtue of their chosen vocation, be virtuosi of language, what most of them actually display is a talent – as unremarkable as it is unrelenting – for mediocre writing; in attempting to distract the reader from their shortcomings, they rely on a panoply of diversionary tactics, from vainglorious obscurity to sensational subject matter. The qualities which, by contrast, make Heaney so deservedly admired include the ability to link evocative words never before found in combination and, indeed, seldom chanced upon in splendid isolation. His ease with words of multiple provenance, from the Gaelic and Anglo-Saxon to the Scots Ulster and Latin; his rooted sense of language as a living dialect; his brio and bravura when it comes to deploying word and trope – these gifts are at the heart of his achievement. There is a radiance about his poems which is an attribute not of his optimism (though he is indubitably more comfortable with celebration than censure) but of the unique space occupied by poems in which the language is revivified and refreshed, renewed and refurbished.

In the satisfyingly loose sequence, 'The Loose Box', the section which deals with grain-threshing is itself like a machine which picks up momentum incrementally, line by line. Soon, however, it has thrummed into life and is generating words 'hard as shot' (to borrow a phrase from his early threshing poem, 'The Wife's Tale') as Heaney recalls, and outshines, the threshing scene in *Tess of the d'Urbervilles*:

> Raving machinery,
> The thresher bucking sky, rut-shuddery,
> A headless Trojan horse expelling straw
> From where the head should be, the underjaws
> Like staircases set champing – it hummed and slugged
> While the big sag and slew of the canvas belt
> That would cut your head off if you didn't watch
> Flowed from the flywheel. And comes flowing back,
> The whole mote-sweaty havoc and mania
> Of threshing day, the feeders up on top
> Like pyre-high Aztec priests gutting forked sheaves
> And paying them ungirded to the drum.

> Slack of gulped straw, the belly-taut of seedbags.
>
> And in the stilly night, chaff piled in ridges,
> Earth raw where the four wheels rocked and battled.

This is high-octane writing of a high order, aided by verbal compounds ('rut-shuddery', 'mote-sweaty', 'sag and slew') and abetted by Heaney's genius at transmuting observation and experience into language of great physical and reverberative precision. A comparable moment of mechanical power in poetry occurs in Ted Hughes's winter poem, 'Tractor', when the frozen machine, finally coaxed into starting, begins 'shuddering itself full of heat'. Characteristically, the Hughes poem is more hit-and-miss than Heaney's; while it contains impressively vigorous language, phrases like 'a more-than-usually-complete materialisation' and 'bursting with superhuman well-being and abandon' leave the tractor rusting in anomalous abstractions rather than gearing up for dynamic action. Heaney's tonal and emotional range in *Electric Light* is evident when 'The Loose Box' is contrasted with 'The Clothes Shrine', a gentle poem – transparent in language and subject matter – which revels in electric light of a less literal kind than the book's title poem. It recalls the 'early years' of marriage to his wife, Marie, and is a perfect instance of Heaney's contention that, through 'poetic technique', an intimate experience can mutate into 'an object to be inspected': 'It calls you close and the intimacy is not embarrassing':

> It was a whole new sweetness
> In the early days to find
> Light white muslin blouses
> On a see-through nylon line
> Drip-drying in the bathroom
> Or a nylon slip in the shine
> Of its own electricity…

The award of the Nobel Prize in Literature in 1995, with all the immense freight of disruption and distraction that will have accompanied it, has not deflected Heaney from his path as a poet who – however allusive and erudite his work may have grown over the years – is drawn to the primal truths at the heart of the everyday. His appetite for poetry and his relish for language are unabated in this post-Nobel collection; individual lines (flower-seed packets are 'sifting lightness and small jittery promise') and individual poems ('The Little Canticles of Asturias' is a bonsai *Divine Comedy*, right down to its final '*stela*'), throughout *Electric Light*, belie the view that poetry can speak to our times only if it is constantly interrogating and ironising its own procedures. His self-questioning tends to be ethically rather than theoretically motivated and, even if we accept that the limits of one's language mark the limits of one's world, Seamus Heaney's language seems so unimpeded, so undaunted, that what his poetry ultimately conveys is a sense of the limitless possibilities of the art.

Having earlier, and with some hesitation, applied to 'Post-script' (the last poem in *The Spirit Level*) Blake Morrison's theory that the final poem of a Heaney collection yields clues to the subsequent collection, I will add a postscript of my own. 'Postscript' is a poem which, taking a cue from its title, the reader may consider separately from the preceding poems in *The Spirit Level*; there is a case, therefore, for contending that it falls to 'Tollund', the penultimate poem in that 1996 collection, to illuminate the reader forward into *Electric Light*. Set in Denmark at the time of the 1994 IRA ceasefire announcement, the poem marks Heaney's first visit to the rural setting of 'The Tollund Man', a 'bog poem' recognised as central to his output since its appearance in *Wintering Out*. At the time of writing 'The Tollund Man' the analogy which was foremost in Heaney's mind was between the Iron Age man (who had been excavated from a Jutland bog) – apparently the sacrificial victim of a violent ritual – and the violence which was rampant in Ulster:

> Out there in Jutland
> In the old man-killing parishes
> I will feel lost,
> Unhappy and at home.

By the time, over twenty years later, 'Tollund' came to be written, 'things had moved on'. The poet (who, typically, seeks analogous Ulster locales – 'It could have been Mulhollandstown or Scribe') is becoming found, happy and at home:

> …it was user-friendly outback
> Where we stood footloose, at home beyond the tribe,
> More scouts than strangers, ghosts who'd walked abroad

> Unfazed by light, to make a new beginning
>
> And make a go of it, alive and sinning,
> Ourselves again, free-willed again, not bad.

Heaney's weighing of his 'responsible *tristia*' reached a peak in the 'Station Island' sequence; after its sombre processions and cathartic professions, he finally began to heed the exhortations of James Joyce's ghost to 'write / for the joy of it', to 'let others wear the sackcloth and the ashes. / Let go, let fly, forget'. He remains a profoundly responsible poet, ever conscious of the artist's overriding commitment to the truth; at the same time, his capacity to 'credit marvels' has found a fresh impetus in the wake of the fragile ceasefire celebrated in 'Tollund'. Admittedly, poems like 'The Border Campaign' and 'Known World' continue his engagement with political subject matter; and 'The Augean Stables', one of the 'Sonnets from Hellas', chillingly records a moment when the 'whitewashed light' of Greece was clouded by news of the sectarian murder of a friend in Ulster. The fact that the friend, Sean Brown, was an athlete (a member, as Heaney himself had been, of the Gaelic Athletic Association or GAA) confers a particular poignancy on the location of the poem in Olympia:

> And it was there in Olympia, down among green willows,
> The lustral wash and run of river shallows,
> That we heard of Sean Brown's murder in the grounds
> Of Bellaghy GAA Club. And imagined
> Hose-water smashing hard back off the asphalt
> In the car park where his athlete's blood ran cold.

Despite the eclogues and other excursions into the pastoral, therefore, death (whether violent or natural) weighs heavily on parts of *Electric Light*. Nonetheless, the 'light' emphasised by Heaney's title animates many of these post-ceasefire poems and there is a 'Tollund'-like lightness to his poetical gait in the mischievous way, for instance, he plays with a title like 'Red, White and Blue'. In previous collections such a title would, in all likelihood, have presaged a politically tinctured poem. Here, the poem's colours are fondly associated with items of clothing worn by Marie during their courtship and the early years of their marriage. The 'hunting-jacket look' of the scarlet coat in the first of the poem's three sections does not prompt references to Yeats's Anglo-Irish world of 'hard-riding country gentlemen' any more than the knights and battlements of 'Castle Childbirth' are used, in the second section, to make a point about foreign conquerors. When, in the third part, the young couple hitch-hiking in the Irish Republic in 1963 are drawn into a sensitive political discussion, they plead 'We're from the north.' Heaney, in this song of innocence, clearly relishes the halcyon memory of a pre-'Troubles' interlude when to be from the north was to be from a place which (discriminatory though it was for Catholics) was not yet synonymous with violence. Although a slighter poem than 'Red, White and Blue', 'Turpin Song' too is notable for its relaxed approach towards potentially political imagery. What makes the poem memorable is its photographically exact evocation of an antique pistol:

> The horse pistol, we called it:
> Brass inlay smooth in the stock,
> Two hammers cocked like lugs,
> Two mottled metal barrels,
> Sooty nostrilled, levelled.

Another possible parallel between *The Spirit Level* and *Electric Light* lies in their respective opening poems, 'The Rain Stick' and 'At Toomebridge'. 'The Rain Stick' is an opening movement that calls for an encore ('Listen now again'); it makes no apology for a second coming – or a thousandth – to familiar Heaney places and themes: 'What happens next / Is undiminished for having happened once, / Twice, ten, a thousand times before.' In this spirit, 'At Toomebridge' recapitulates earlier Heaney poems (including 'A Lough Neagh Sequence' in *Door Into the Dark*, 'Toome' in *Wintering Out* and 'The Toome Road' in *Field Work*). Acting as a 'You Are Here' sign, the poem berths the poet securely at the start of this peripatetic collection in a known and loved place – a place at which turbulent currents of history ('Where the checkpoint used to be. / Where the rebel boy was hanged in '98') are counterpointed by the 'continuous present' of the Bann River, and where 'negative ions in the open air / Are poetry to me'. A poem almost as short and cryptic as a 'gloss', 'At Toomebridge' anticipates that same seamless weave of time evident elsewhere in the collection ('All that was written / And to come I was a part of then') and might be echoing 'The Rain Stick', as well as reprising the eel imagery of 'A Lough Neagh Sequence', when it ends: 'As once before / The slime and silver of the fattened eel'.

Like Patrick Kavanagh, Heaney is aware that to get to know one small field takes a lifetime's exploration. Yet, however distant he may have grown, through time and travel, from the first field – perhaps the 'field behind the house' where he was lost among the pea-drills as a child – it remains a real place, to which he is permanently bound: a touchstone for authenticity and a fertile source of vision. As he writes in 'The Loose Box', in lines which again carry a faint echo of Shakespeare ('Now would I give a thousand furlongs of sea for an acre of barren ground: long heath, broom, furze, anything'):

> On an old recording Patrick Kavanagh states
> That there's health and worth in any talk about
> The properties of land. Sandy, glarry,
> Mossy, heavy, cold, the actual soil
> Almost doesn't matter; the main thing is
> An inner restitution, a purchase come by
> By pacing it in words that make you feel
> You've found your feet in what 'surefooted' means
> And in the ground of your own understanding…

A book of present and past, multiple births and manifold deaths, of eidetic evocations and sophisticated allusions, of the lambently local and the urbanely international, Electric Light shows Heaney still eluding categorisation, still shirking a 'last definition'. To paraphrase 'A Norman Simile' (one of the 'Ten Glosses'), he is marvellously himself; and the poems in this collection – in the punning words which conclude 'The Clothes Shrine' – are 'got through / As usual, brilliantly'. A further 'gloss' which it is apposite to quote is 'The Bridge': remove the title, and you are left with a riddle; remove the bridge and you are looking at the poet himself:

> Steady under strain and strong through tension,
> Its feet on both sides but in neither camp,
> It stands its ground, a span of pure attention,

> A holding action, the arches and the ramp
> Steady under strain and strong through tension.
>
> *Parnassus,* Vol. 26 No. 2 (2002)

Reprinted with kind permission from Denis O'Driscoll, *The Outnumbered Poet: Critical and Autobiographical Essays,* The Gallery Press, 2013.

*Peter McDonald*

## A Night Sky

1

If ever, now; now would be the right time,
when nothing ever after could be worse:
the sky drained, ready for the moon to climb,
with small birds raucous, and the pigeons terse;
if ever a day's heat could end in cold,
and the night-winds bring on a day of rain;
if there was ever a moment to be bold
and face outright the things that are all pain;

if ever, now: but now their strength has gone
from more than the last sunlight and the sky,
courage has little left to settle on,
and all its sounds make one unearthly cry:
there's nothing left, either to join or sever,
make whole or take to pieces now, if ever.

2

Like somebody who sees, or thinks he sees,
past layers of thin cloud in the early night
a new moon rising, I begin to tease
a shape out from the far edge of my sight
and turn it into you, as you might look
apart from life, where reflections slip faint
outlines around a form, maybe the fluke
image of you, with their frail tint and taint.

Much as clouds thicken, sadness makes the lines
blur, lose themselves, fall back, steadily fade
to what could pass for nothing, and outshines
only the shadows solid bodies make:
its half-glow strengthens almost to a blink,
then leaves a ghost-light to recede and sink.

3

Twice every day, cold water in the sea
covers a causeway over rocks and weed,
at low tide walkable and slippery
light-coloured sandstone, three or four feet wide,
up to an unmanned lighthouse just offshore,
a path that comes and vanishes and comes
again in all weathers, a half-sunk floor
between crags where the wind warbles and hums.

Returning regular as day and night,
remorse, isolate, strides down the high road
with cries and calls between distress and spite,
to take whatever payment might be owed:
desire and lack are all it wails and raves;
no respite but the chilly, rising waves.

4

Shy of the daylight, animals unseen
to us work through their decay and their prime;
winter and summer and the months between
turn into each other for the umpteenth time
and still from black-wrapped trees and hidden holes
in earth, the foxes and the owls embark
to search out in their desperate patrols
nightwalking victims, cautious in the dark.

The silence makes me hear things, makes me hear
you, and whatever the sounds you were trying
to pick out, off-key, high as if with fear,
from far off when the spirits you heard crying
were all the hunted creatures, innocent,
gone to their deaths long since, never silent.

5

I know that I should say the better thing
to you, although poor reasons could be tried
to plead a cause, show new bruises, and bring
you for a while to something like my side;
I know exactly what you need to hear
and the hard detail of what's to be told,
final and reeling, as when sun rakes clear
whole fields of stone and brambles in the cold.

And yet I know I needn't tell you this,
for you can see me now, in flat daylight,
like a target impossible to miss
struck over and over in a fair fight:
whoever leaves me sprawling on the floor
will love you better, I know, if not more.

6

Remember that the soul cannot return
and, if it did, would not be welcomed back;
its lightest footsteps, so hard to discern
on the bare roads, and the true sound they lack,
are things the better now for having vanished
into the further stretches of each night
where nothing waits for the weak spirit, banished
to an offshore rock, a long-abandoned light:

it breathes sea-water and breathes cutting wind,
manning a station at the edge of death,
all warmth gone with the blood it left behind,
more distant than lost love, or living breath.
The waves are blacker where the light would fall:
remembering this, you can forget it all.

7

Her turn now to say nothing, turn aside
like a wronged spirit hearing talk in hell
from the lover who betrayed her once and lied,
sorry and voluble to no avail;
her turn to scorn with silence, and rejoin
a past he never asked about, where now
for ever she belongs, and where her pain
is nothing he can disown or allow.

The last he sees of her is her black hair
going into the dark, going too soon;
he can no more reach out and touch her there
than touch a night sky without stars or moon,
no more hear her than listen to the cries
of stones, grievous with their own weight and size.

8

I wanted to dig through topsoil to clay,
knowing there would be nothing, knowing there
would be only the weight as it gave way
under my weight, this ground hard to lay bare;
I wanted to peel back with my own hands
layers that stuck and crumbled, and so toil
away that legs and feet could give commands
against thick stones and dead roots in the soil;

and yet their straining orders went unheeded
until the very shovel seemed to bend,
for all the push to get to what I needed
was pushed against, and wasted in the end:
it was my strength at fault, a never-daunted
courage that ruined all I ever wanted.

## 9

Not once did I put anything away
for fear of the blunt hurt that it would do;
nothing that I could give back or unsay
did I return or say again to you;
not once did the bright surfaces of things
taken as fragile, intricate, no more,
seem any the less bright for what time brings,
knowing they were all broken at the core;

instead, I kept their brittle pieces close
together, and I watched them, without hope
or pleasure, just watched them, numb and morose,
my face struck by the hard end of a rope
still knotted, whose blind force could lay me flat:
not once, but times past number I did that.

## 10

The line between unhappiness and joy,
recrossed so often, was no more a line
than the pen in my hand was only a toy
when it found lies and fantasies to sign
my name to; no more than the line between
imagining and laying down the law,
shading away the truth and coming clean,
between what I saw and I thought I saw:

there was a difference, impossible
to picture or locate; there was a change
somewhere I couldn't name, but I could tell
that it had come, that everything was strange
I'd ever known, all sorrow, yet no more
sorrow than happiness had been before.

## 11

The dawn frost like a bloom across flat ground;
jet-trails over the sky like shallow scores;
thorn hedges like wires tangled and unwound;
cars closing on us fast like slamming doors;
the first blow like a hammer to the heart;
the pressure of a hand like taken breath;
cold air like famine, prising lives apart;
long fences broken like the gates of death;

like you and me, the ghosts that walk these lanes;
like winter wind, the blast of memory;
like portraits, the half-icy windowpanes;
like flimsy litter, leaves as they work free:
the future and the past, like drought and dearth,
here dazzle, but like nothing on this earth.

## 12

I half expect to meet her coming back
here at the entrance to the cul-de-sac,
though she will scarcely recognise the child
whose look must puzzle her, who never left
this place, still at the door of a red-tiled
hall, and just staring, silently bereft.

This must be when I fall in love with her
in the full light of a drizzly cold day,
on a stone path that's damaged past repair,
its ground never imaginable-away,
where I watch in her eyes only the dark
that must come in between us, both apart,
to bring a night sky without star or spark:
I see the end, even here at the start.

*Dilys Rose*

# Swansdown and Diamante

A night in November. Cold. Wet. Shiny pavements. A seethe of starlings. Miles was off to The Alhambra, via a quick pre-show snifter with Johnny Brock, an often cited but rarely seen acquaintance. On the drive to town, he'd been as fidgety as a boy on a first date, checking his appearance in the rearview mirror, tipping his new hat – a charcoal fedora – this way and that, adjusting the knot on his garish kipper tie, straightening his collar, patting the breast pocket of his corduroy jacket, checking far too often that he had his ticket.

Gala and Gran were going to the ballet at The King's: Gran's treat, for Gala doing well in her ballet exam. As they crossed the road, leaning into the driving rain, Gran slithered on the wet cobbles, lost her balance, and clutched Gala's arm.

Dearie me, she said, righting herself. Near a goner there. Skiting aboot like a clown. Is this us?

Must be. There's the prima ballerina.

Gran scanned the street.

Whereaboots?

On the poster!

Aye, aye, right ye are.

The prima ballerina couldn't be on the street right now, Gran. She'll be in her dressing room, doing her make-up.

Silly old me. But she's lovely, isn't she? Lovely.

They joined the queue outside the theatre. Umbrellas lined the building like a border of black, densely packed shrubs. Orange lightbulbs picked out the words *The King's Theatre* and reflections thrown back by shiny pavements gave a warm glow to the pallid faces of those in the queue. A man with an accordion approached. His face was red raw, his clothes soaked through. From his battered instrument, he squeezed out a harsh bleating, like a sheep caught on barbed wire. Gran greeted him with her warmest smile.

Now that's a bonny tune, son. Where have I heard that afore? To Gala she whispered: Look in ma handbag, dear. Can you see ma purse?

The man was skinny as a whippet. The smell which came off him was like a sour shield. His fingers fumbled and slithered over the keys, hitting wrong notes galore. It was hard to tell how the tune was meant to sound or if he was even playing a tune at all; he might as well have been making it up as he went along. He didn't say anything, just kept squeezing away, standing directly in front of Gala, looking straight through her as if she were made of glass.

Gie the fella a shillin, dear, said Gran. I'm sure there's a shillin in ma purse. He'll mibbe hae a family tae feed. If no, he'll hae plenty ither ways tae part wi it.

A shilling, Gala thought, was a lot to hand over on account of such an awful racket.

Gie the fella a shillin, dear.

Reluctantly Gala held out the coin. The man's hand flew off his instrument, plucked the coin from her fingers and slipped it into his waistcoat pocket, with the speed and sleight of Artful Arcady performing one of his card tricks. He gave the barest of nods, so minimal it might just have been a twitch, then moved off down the queue.

They were way up in the gods, close to the ceiling where plaster cherubs, with mischievous amusement, surveyed the audience. The seats were so high up and the rows so steeply raked that Gala felt her centre of gravity shift, tilt, as if at the slightest knock she might topple over the rail, roll and bounce across the Grand Circle, flip over its ornate rail and thud into the stalls; bruised and battered and possibly dead.

Gran passed over a bag of sweeties. The house lights dipped and the tilting subsided.

Take a couple the now so we dinny crackle once the show's on the go.

The first half was extracts from *Swan Lake* and *Giselle*. Ballerinas in feathery tutus with muscly legs and flat chests picked about on *pointes*, hair scraped back and covered with feather caps or set off by tiaras. The male dancers, in white tights, displayed bulging thighs and groins. They strode, or leapt, or supported ballerinas in arabesques and pirouettes. It was all graceful and shapely. The music was sad and passionate. After a while, though Gala still clung to remnants of the 'When I grow up I want to be a ballerina' fantasy, she became just a little bored. The moves were repetitive, the acting hammy. The men looked unlike any men she'd ever seen in the poses they struck: the arrow clearly didn't pierce the swan princess's heart and she collapsed far too elegantly for somebody who had been mortally wounded.

After the interval, during which she and Gran licked vanilla ice cream off flat little wooden spoons, then took turns to use the programme as a fan, the curtain rose once more on a stage flooded with red light. The set was a cocktail bar. Women in slinky red dresses lounged around on high stools or leaned against pillars, rearranging their limbs, smoking cigarettes and drinking from long-stemmed, wide-brimmed glasses. Red, black, and the pinkish white which went by the name of 'flesh-coloured' featured extensively. Not all the flesh-coloured areas were an illusion created by body-stockings and tights: some of them, quite a lot in fact, were bare skin.

I think we're in some sorta bordello! Gran whispered. Wi women o ill repute!

The music was smoky and jazzy. The female dancers did a lot of close, slithery moves with each other and with the men. Nobody was on *pointes*. No arabesques or pirouettes were executed with consummate skill. There was no pining for absent lovers, no tragic but unconvincing deaths. There were, however, a number of jealous lovers and rough, almost realistic fighting.

The atmosphere was tense. At one point a man grabbed one of the women and tried to kiss her. She pushed him away. He grabbed her again, roughly, pushing her head back and yanking her by the hair. She struggled, he grabbed her again. This time he tore at her dress, ripped it right off. The woman acted upset but didn't do anything to cover herself up and she wasn't even wearing a bra. She was topless! And stayed topless right up to the final curtain.

Dearie me, said Gran with a quavery giggle, as they joined the exodus stepping down the eternal, winding staircase from the gods, that wis a bit racy!

The rain beat on the car roof. Gala's father, fedora at a rakish angle, gripped the steering wheel with both hands, peered through the streaming windscreen at the hazy road ahead.

Marvellous! he said. Bloody marvellous!

You got yir money's worth, then? said Gran.

You can say that again. Three encores. Three! Worth every penny. *Outside the barracks, in the pouring rain* – I'd happily sit through it all over again – *Falling in love again, never wanted to, what am I to do, I can't help it.*

My word, said Gran. Ye'd better no let Vera hear that. She'll fair take the hump.

Might make her pull her socks up. Sorry, Lottie. Forget I said that. Mum's the word, eh? Bloody hell!

He swerved just in time to avoid a parked car.

Of all the stupid places to park! Impossible to see, especially in this weather – *I'm warm again, my pack is light, it's you, Lili Marleen, it's you Lili Marleen.*

I like that yin, said Gran. Catchy. But sad, tae. Reminds me o the Blitz.

A night to remember! A once-in-a-lifetime experience!

His voice outdid the rain.

And did Johnny Brock enjoy the show?

Oh yes. I'd say every full-blooded man in the audience enjoyed the show immensely. More men than women in the audience, you know. And some of the women were – he lowered his voice – the *short back and sides* variety. In *trouser suits*!

Dearie me, said Gran.

And between you and me – he lowered his voice again and of course Gala listened more closely – there was a rather sizeable contingent of *nancy boys*, swanking around, brazen as all come out.

Marlene's aye been popular wi aw sorts, said Gran.

Don't know what the world's coming to when that sort can go parading around, happy as Larry.

They're aw God's children. Anybody for a chocolate raisin? said Gran, rustling her poke of sweeties.

Too much *license* these days, too much *libertarianism*, he continued. We should never have done away with National Service.

Och, dinny let ony o that spoil yir night, Miles.

A good dose of discipline would knock those limp-wristed Jessies into shape.

So whit were the great lady's costumes like? Did Marlene wear lovely dresses?

Gowns. Gorgeous gowns. The acme of glamour. Diamante from top to toe. Marvellous. And that swansdown cloak has to be seen to be believed. And how was the ballet?

Lovely, said Gran. We had a grand time, didn't we?

It was great. We were so high up we could almost touch the angels on the ceiling.

I don't have much time for ballet, myself, said Miles. Men in tights prancing around.

They were only in tights for the first bit, said Gala. After that the men wore proper trousers.

Good thing too, if you ask me. Men in tights! Leaves no room for the imagination.

The rain streamed down the windscreen. The wipers clicked back and forth at top speed but were having little effect. Street lights were a fuzz of yellow, traffic lights a smear of green, amber, red.

*Falling in love again,* her father sang, *never wanted to, what am I to do, I caaaaaan't help it.*

---

'Swansdown and Diamante' is an extract from *Pelmanism*, forthcoming from Luath Press.

# Ciaran Carson

## Follain Poems

*Author's Note: These poems are part of a book called* From Elsewhere, *to be published by The Gallery Press in 2014. Those with French/ English titles are my translations of poems by Jean Follain (1903–1971); those with English titles are my response to the translations, whether spins on them, or takes on them. In other words, they form a dialogue of sorts.*

### Le calme: The Calm

The image on the wall
shows God emerging from the clouds.
The sound of a pen
in this long narrow
country office
echoes from afar
after the wars.
The mud of the marshes beyond
barely stirs
a hand advances
to seize a rabbit
which will die there and then.
In a tree in full leaf
a squirrel hears the cries
and does not understand the broken calm.

# The Word

If according to the proverb
God sees the black insect
passing on the black stone
how much more does He see
the boy's hand stealing forth
to pluck the apple
from the apple-box
or the red insect falling
into the chalice to commune
with the communion wine
at the moment of its being
turned into blood by the uttering of a word.

# Poursuite: Pursuit

Rust eats right
into the spear head
horses dwell in silence
though the hunt is on
for this man
who runs alone through
labyrinths and ruins
for he never could
reconcile himself to these times.

# Missing

Mushroom after seeming
mushroom leads the seeker ever
deeper than he has
been into the woods
two days gone
sounds of helicopter, dog, jeep,
by night thronged
with searchlights
shouts and horns
as for the difference
between mushroom
and toadstool
what would life be
without uncertainty

## Visionnaire: Visionary

The bones of the head throb
the village of an evening
swimming in alcohol
the monstrance
scintillating in the church
when a being enters into trance
in a kitchen piled high
with earthenware and pewterware
and meat and bread
in the surrounding farmlands
each ear of wheat is gorged with night
and the rats in the granaries
tremble with fear in the fullness of life.

# According to Scripture

The granaries are filled with black wheat
the rain-barrels frozen solid
but the saviour shall come
to be honoured
among the beasts of the field
among hyenas and ostriches
among the dragons and the owls
he shall be honoured
because he gave water in the desert
and floods in the wilderness
a company of pale millers
marches on the village
where the men castrate sows.

# Viande noire: Black Meat

Around precious stones
which grind nothing but
their own dust
the eaters cut into
their black meat
the trees on the horizon
are contoured
like a monumental sentence
images are transfigured
as light leaks away piecemeal
there is a noise of venison
being chewed.
In each and every thing
deepness fattens.

# The Hunters

A mile beyond the great bay
window two wives
holding glasses of wine
stare out from into the dark
mist rises from the lake
amid the forest
two husbands who have lost
their quarry
let off their guns at
one and the same time
out on the estuary
two ships sound their foghorns
in and out of sync
then vanish.

*David Wheatley*

# The Commissar of Castle House: On Dennis O'Driscoll

Dennis O'Driscoll died on Christmas Eve 2012, a week shy of what would have been his fifty-ninth birthday. The news found me in an arctically cold rented house in Aberdeen, whither I had moved a few days previously. That summer I had celebrated getting a new job in that city by sending Dennis a postcard portrait of his friend George Mackay Brown; any reply he sent was most likely at the bottom of the shanty town of cardboard boxes among which I now lived. At his funeral, I watched a shaken Seamus Heaney deliver a pained and faltering eulogy. Revisiting the cemetery in Naas the following autumn, I found a stone on Dennis's grave on which someone had painted the line (from his posthumously published *Dear Life*), 'I had it seems unknown to me been living my life to the full.' *Dear Life* was his ninth collection, if we count *Foreseeable Futures*, the collection with which he concludes his *New and Selected Poems* in 2004; his first, *Kist*, was published by Dolmen Press in 1982. In 2001 he raided his incomparable back catalogue of reviews and articles for *Troubled Thoughts, Majestic Dreams*, a volume of selected prose. When Seamus Heaney won the Nobel Prize for Literature in 1995, Dennis's pickings and choosings column in *Poetry Ireland Review* proved its Argus-like credentials by ferreting out the reaction of *The Farmer's Journal* ('Bellaghy Celebrates as Farmer's Son Wins Top Literary Award'). Dennis's way with a quotation reminded me of Walter Benjamin, who dreamed of assembling a book entirely from quotations; Dennis did just that with his *Bloodaxe Book of Poetry Quotations* in 2006. Two years later, he coaxed from Heaney the proxy memoir that may not otherwise have got written, the invaluable *Stepping Stones*. Now he is gone, and almost a year after his death comes *The Outnumbered Poet: Critical and Autobiographical Essays*, published by The Gallery Press.

The last time I saw Dennis – that sounds uncomfortably close to a Joni Mitchell lyric, doesn't it – was in New York in November 2011, at an event in the Irish Arts Center in Manhattan. He and I contributed to a Thomas Kinsella tribute event mentioned here in 'The Poetry of Bureaucracy: Thomas Kinsella's Two Careers'. Drawing on interviews with that poet and his fellow civil servant T.K. Whitaker, Dennis describes the continuity rather than conflict the young Kinsella experienced in combining his job at the Lemass-era Department of Finance with his burgeoning poetic career. He would spend the day organising one kind of material, he tells Dennis, then came home and continue in the same vein. The symbiosis of Dennis's day-job and his poetry is a topic he too ventilated in print, many times. One of the more amusing moments in *The Outnumbered Poet* occurs when Richard Murphy introduces Dennis to Susan Sontag as someone who embodied T.S. Eliot's belief that a poet 'should have a job', a suggestion that prompts some bristling from the American. In an essay on Michael Hartnett, Dennis describes the Munster's poet fondness for long telephone conversations, part of whose appeal must have been the certainty of finding Dennis at his desk. If his work as a customs and excise man involved international toings and froings, his calls from the lobby involved plenty of cosmopolitan traffic too, as when Heaney turned up in the company of Czesław Miłosz. Or do I mean Joseph Brodsky? It takes six steps to get to Kevin Bacon in the parlour game, but with Dennis connections tended to be direct; small wonder then if the cast of my Dennis anecdotes is so embarrassingly star-studded and difficult to keep track of. Those last two poets had their brushes with secret policemen, but in Dennis they found a fellow poetry partisan fighter with the best filing system this side of the Stasi.

Here, though, a basic difference between Kinsella and Dennis suggests itself. Despite his association with that arch-moderniser T.K. Whitaker and reputation as a Pound-friendly broadener of Irish horizons, Kinsella's poetry responded to the opening up of Irish society in the 60s with a curious contractile defensiveness. In 'Nightwalker', two German investors are treated with suspicion, between their predatory interest in Irish art and sudden (and badly misjudged) metamorphosis into concentration camp guards, of all things. As for Kinsella the critic, his interest in contemporary poetry – or poetry of a more recent vintage than Austin Clarke, at any rate – has been perfunctory. Dennis's response to social change, on the merry-go-round from post-Haughey economic doldrums to prosperity and back again, was expansive and engaged (and not without satirical claws), from the first stirrings of *nouveau riche arrivisme* in *Weather Permitting* (1997) all the way to the sad post-Celtic Tiger ps and signing off of *Dear Life* (2012). And where Dennis the critic is concerned, it hardly requires the appearance of *The Outnumbered Poet* to remind us of what we have lost, but here goes anyway. In the republic of poetry, no commissar ranked higher; none matched his hawk-like overview, his talent-spotting (first critic in Europe to write about Les Murray); his cynicism-free generosity and indefatigability; and, to wax Heideggerian about it, his *Dasein*, his simply being there, whether at his desk in the Castle, at the end of a phone line or a postcard, or in dozens of reviews, carefully snipped out and tucked into the relevant slim volumes – clippings that, often enough, retain their interest long after that of the books themselves has palled.

*The Outnumbered Poet* divides, like *Ulysses*, into a long central section flanked by a shorter introit and *nunc dimittis*. Section one begins with 'Walking Out', an edgy portrait of the midlands Irish town of Naas. Passing an empty hotel dining room, Dennis's eye is caught by a sartorially impeccable waiter, whom he furnishes with an imagined bored nostalgia for 'a tower block in outer Vilnius or a log cottage in sylvan Belarus'. As ever with Dennis, we have the 'importance of elsewhere' (*La double vie de Dennis*, to put it in Kieślowskian terms) and an undertow of 'home is so sad', but the Larkin comparison is missing at least one dimension. A poet well served by Dennis, Larkin comes to an eloquent accommodation with his adoptive city in the 1982 anthology *A Rumoured City*: 'Hull is still as good a place to write as any. Better, in fact, than some. For a place cannot produce poems: it can only not prevent them, and Hull is good at that.' Dennis's evocation of Naas makes no such allowance for its poetically sustaining qualities, not even of the work-life-balance kind one might have expected from a commuter poet. Though undated, 'Walking Out' appears to have been written after Dennis's early retirement from the civil service. The headcount of reprinted shorter reviews in *The Outnumbered Poet* is lower than in its 2001 precursor, *Troubled Thoughts, Majestic Dreams*, and noticing the falling off in Dennis's reviewing in the years before his death I wondered what was behind it. The answer, I now see, is that he was exploring longer (in some cases much longer) essays, many of which are effectively mini-memoirs.

The reviewer's primary impulse, to pan the living stream for the precious metal among the dross, has not disappeared, however. A perennial challenge for the review as a genre is whether a collection of impressionistic responses can achieve the larger purchase on the text required to write or rewrite literary history. A certain forcefulness is required for the requisite escape velocity, though there will always be reviewers for whom the formula 'Not all the poems in this book are equally successful' represents the *ne plus ultra* of objurgation. Is it the critic's job to respond exclusively to what is in front of him or her, to plod dutifully through the prize shortlists in the hope the kiddies will have tried a little harder than usual this year? Or is something more astringent called for? There is also, for the writer who's been in the business for decades, the challenge of keeping it up (Dennis's first reviews appeared in *Hibernia* in the early 70s, where they made enough of an impression for UCC Professor Seán Lucy to write in demanding his sacking). Noticing one's age as a critic is not unlike noticing how young policemen are getting these days, but there comes a point where scything down one's juniors (not a review-style much practised by Dennis, it should be said) takes on an air of unseemliness, while the alternative risks looking like handing out lollipops to schoolchildren. The catastrophe, Walter Benjamin said, is that things just keep rolling along, and there are signs throughout *The Outnumbered Poet* of a critic keen to rethink his *métier* and work on a broader canvas, and rejecting the Tetris games the reviewer is increasingly forced to play with the public prints still prepared to tolerate his presence.

Consequently, 'Blurbonic Plague' takes up very much where Dennis left off with 'Pen Pals: Insider Dealing in Poetry Futures' in *Troubled Thoughts, Majestic Dreams*. Blurbs are 'fibbing', 'dissembling', 'mealy-mouthed' and 'weasel-worded', their writers less unacknowledged legislators than 'grubbing copywriters', 'abusing the very language they purport to purify'. Intense stuff, and in no time we are into a bottom-line analysis of poetry publishing today, in the same vein as Matthew Sperling's 'Books and the Market' in Peter Robinson's *Oxford Handbook of Contemporary British and Irish Poetry*. Thinking about the state of poetry publishing today and how to fix it, one has the impression of stitching up a raggedy armrest on a sofa while the repossession men pick it and you up and carry you out of the house. If the axing of the Oxford poetry list suggested the unsustainability of poetry-publishing for an uncommitted non-specialist press, the implosion of the Salt list exposed the limits of supply-side overproduction, as a generation of creative writing MA graduates broke into print without any accompanying readership to sustain them. 'Like the shopping in a bypassed town, the regular browsing of the poetry shelves is largely the preserve of locals: poets themselves or those embarked on writing or studying verse', Dennis writes. As things stand, the distinction between poets and non-poets browsing the next-to-non-existent poetry section of a doomed bookshop may be a moot one. True, the worse things get the more imperative it becomes that we cultivate the few real critics left – that scattered, rag-tag battalion – but the malaise is endemic and structural, not an incidental side-effect of what a generous host of souls today's blurbers are. (Feeling its lack in the previous sentence, I hereby propose 'a frothing' as the relevant collective noun.)

Yet for all the righteousness of his indignation, there is something elliptical about Dennis's ire. Though his principal target is the institutionalised blurbitis of US publishing, where MFA teachers turn up on the back of their students' books like anxious parents at a school sports day, it has achieved a calamitous hold on UK and Irish publishing too. Not a few of the larger publishers deface the backs of debut collections with well-wishers' sentiments that would not disgrace a Christmas card but have no business in print. The practice is patronising and abhorrent, but Dennis forbears from naming names. Why? The sleaziness of the poetry world genuinely pained Dennis, I have no doubt, but he was not one for the retributive pub-talk to which most other poets (the present writer included) resort, in or out of print. Nor was he the kind of critic who saw X for the monster of nepotism he/she is and held it vengefully against his/her excellence as a poet, where such is the case. In Dennis's presence, Seamus Heaney said in his funeral eulogy for him, 'it was impossible to say or do anything base', and my suspicion is that he chose the high-minded route in the hope of gently coaxing the rest of us in the same direction, and out of the Malebolge of gang or playground warfare that is British and Irish poetry today. And that's just the backs of books. The world of the internet came a little too late for Dennis, but in so far as he was aware of the bacchanalia of self-promotion to be found on poets' websites and social media pages, he found it distressing and incomprehensible. Why would anyone go on the internet to talk about their own poetry?

Perhaps it was the intractability of these questions and what they mean for the future of poetry that pushed Dennis towards memoir. Often, essays morph into memoir without warning, as when a piece on Yehuda Amichai turns into the aforementioned recollections of Susan Sontag. Often, Dennis's poets are observed in small groups, with some unexpected results, as when R.S. Thomas is introduced to Miłosz. The Pole was aware of the Welshman's work, but Thomas did not read poetry in translation ('Penguin did terrible harm by publishing all those Europeans', he pronounces.) There is an essay of Larkin's on A.E. Housman called 'All Right When You Knew Him', and Dennis's portrait of Thomas prises the grimacing mask of Old Testament Prophet off the Welsh poet's features, revealing a rather different creature underneath. Few people, I suspect, will read Thomas's fulminations on the evils of microwave ovens and the desirability of airplanes falling out of the sky without feeling that they are in the presence of a contrived performance – one that allowed the poet-priest the double benefit of keeping journalists at bay and pleasantly surprising people when he turned out, in person, not to be quite the dog-collared Robespierre of the valleys they had expected. The presence of his second wife Betty at the Miłosz-Thomas pow-wow, deflating his outbursts with an interjected 'Rubbish!' or 'Watch it!', also does its bit for the general bonhomie in the air at the Shelbourne Hotel. Conviviality does not blunt Dennis's critical faculties, and in their roundabout way these sociable essays are full of sharp and unexpected insights. Dennis had patently little time for the post-*Howl* Ginsberg and his Blake-impersonating party-trick, we learn, and was equally unimpressed by Hugh MacDiarmid's 'sanguinary' Stalinism of two decades before. Not that these dislikes come down to those writers' leftism: he revered Bertolt Brecht this side idolatry, a passion he is at pains to impress on Czesław Miłosz. Joseph Brodsky's McGonagallesque impersonation of a globe-trotting Nobel laureate, prize and all, also leaves Dennis cold.

For all the back-slapping, puerility and general idiocy of literary chit-chat, no one ever shouted, or needed to shout 'Rubbish!' at Dennis in conversational mid-flow. The sense of occasion never flags or descends into self-serving small talk. In 'My First Acquaintance With Poets', Hazlitt describes rising before daybreak to walk ten miles in the mud to hear Coleridge preach. Faithfully picking up visitors from ferry terminals and railway stations in *The Outnumbered Poet*, Dennis was just as ceremonial about a chance meeting in the street, which he might then follow up with a careful postcard, as though thanking one for a dinner party weeks in the planning. The combination of the ambulatory-accidental and the sit-down high-serious is all very Joycean, and is a feature too of the longest essay here, on Michael

Hartnett. This piece is exceptional not just for its wealth of biographical and critical detail (it is surely the best thing ever written on that poet), but also for its unembarrassed weighing of that poet's masterly but uneven body of work. Here is Dennis on *A Farewell to English*, that most emotive and wrongheaded of Hartnett's books: 'A jumble of caricature and sentimentality, appallingly ill-advised attempts at political satire that combine the cheapest of shots with the crudest of analogies, and wrongheaded rants against Yeats and his successors.' In the very failures of these poems, as so unstintingly diagnosed here, Hartnett embodies something about the problems of the Yeatsian inheritance for poets from the Republic – a category that includes Dennis himself, born fifteen years after Yeats's death. Behind the Yeatsian vision of Ireland, there is, let us concede, a highly personal act of mythmaking. Having recognised this, a writer might see it as an enabling fiction – enabling for Yeats, at least, but one that future generations would attempt to reproduce at their peril. What we witness in 'A Farewell to English', however, is the Yeatsian legacy crushing the life out of a lesser poet unable to match it with a myth of anything like the same potency. Instead, he falls back on a narrative of community (or worse, racial) identity, with Yeats on the wrong side of the tribal divide, flogging off the commodified Celtic soul to impressionable Yanks. Dennis fairly excoriates the failings of this position, and understandably so. Its Corkeryan retro-trip is disastrous not only for its reactionary politics, but its misguided attempt to will important poetry into being by way of ideology. (It is revealing that the poems in this vein in *A Farewell to English* are markedly more misguided and worse than those actually *in* Irish that followed.) On the subject of America, nay-sayers have suggested that America spoils Irish poets, inducing hypertrophy of the slim volume as surely as that of the waistband, but Dennis reminds us of the spilling over of Hartnett's racial rhetoric into his protest poem 'USA', with its dubious defence of Native Americans, pitting 'pure blood' versus 'dubious bastard stocks'. Book by book (since Hartnett's unevenness was very much a book-by-book, rather than early-versus-late affair) Dennis sifts, disposes of the dross and redirects us to the undervalued riches. It is rare indeed to witness a critic so lovingly defend a poet against himself: Hartnett worked as a telephonist, and at moments like this it is as though the chatter in Buswell's Hotel bar has been connected on a direct line to posterity.

I don't always find myself in agreement with Dennis, I must confess. Billy

Collins is one of the great attention-seekers of our time, forever jabbing a finger in the reader's ribs or tugging at our shirtsleeve to remind us what an agreeable fellow he is. Like Dennis, I don't mind saluting Collins' aversion to 'mask[ing] vacuity with obscurity', if only because I don't think he's masking it with anything at all. It's interesting to find Dennis using his review of Collins to float a theory of poetic diction, in which Eliot's defence of difficulty is symptomatic of his 'profound personal turmoil' in the 1920s and its afterlife in the 'tranquil environment' of creative writing programmes has become a joyless avant-garde production line. Interesting, since by and large Dennis avoids era-wide generalisations (though modernism and the contemporary avant-garde were never among his favourite things), but also for how the rejection of modernism awards Collins the stewardship of a natural, lyric tradition holding the line in the face of insurgent avant-garde cadres. This makes me uneasy on two counts. First, because I don't see Collins as the natural evolutionary successor to Eliot or other leftover saurians from pre-Movement times. And second, because I find his winsome slim volumes (winsome, lose some as Alan Bennett said) so paltry in comparison to those of Eliot, Stevens, Moore, Auden, Berryman and the other poets that shaped me, as a teenager, and can't see any amount of Collins' footling whimsy as a good enough reason for trading one style for the other. Ours has been a more egalitarian age than pre-war days, but how lucky an age for poetry has it been? 'Let us not then speak ill of our generation,' Pozzo tells himself disconsolately in *Waiting for Godot*, even if all he then finds to say in its favour is: 'It is true the population has increased.'

I spoke of community, or the idea of community, as one antidote to Yeats's eccentric mythopoeia. Ours is a communitarian age, and in few institutions is this more apparent than the poetry reading. There was a time when inviting a poet into a school or a seminar room carried a moderate to high risk of bad behaviour, whether sexual or alcoholic, but woe betide the poet today unable to follow up a debut collection with the requisitely professional reading-plus-workshop act that is now the basic unit of currency on the creative writing circuit. 'The Outnumbered Poet: Poets and Poetry Readings' offers an enjoyable refresher course in the follies of poetic performance. Its title comes from Thomas Lynch's quip that any reading where the audience outnumber the people onstage counts as a success. Dennis cites the unsuccessful reading described in Tomás Ó Criomthain's *An t-Oileánach*, where Ó Criomthain is subjected to a tedious recitation by the island poet, but is too tactful to ask him to stop. It's one step up, I suppose, from the village poet in Bohumil Hrabal's *Too Loud a Silence*, who holds a knife to the necks of passer-bys, recites his poetry, then explains it's the only way he's found to get people to listen to him. All humanity's problems stem from us not being able to sit alone in our rooms, said Pascal. A large subset of these problems stem from the associated problem of poets not having worked out that the invention of the book makes their work available to read by the general public, in silence, alone. It is more than a little poignant, then, to see Dennis quote Juvenal, Leopardi, Myles na gCopaleen and Peter Reading on the horrors of poetry readings, given his own saintly powers of endurance where these performances were concerned. Still, all that time can't have been entirely wasted if it inspired the windy bore of his comic gem 'The Next Poem' ('This poem has gone down extremely well in Swedish translation… You have to picture it set out on the page as five sonnet-length trapezoids…'). One of the reasons Larkin preferred consuming poems on the page rather than at readings, he insisted, was that at least on the page you know when they're going to end.

It is this quality of infinite forbearance that springs to mind most often when I think of Dennis. Was he too tolerant, too lacking in the bile and *sprezzatura* that may indeed be what our age deserves? 'They will come no more, /The old men with beautiful manners', Ezra Pound wrote of 'I Vecchi' in 'Moeurs Contemporaines', not that Dennis lived to be properly old (I write this on what would have been his sixtieth birthday, 1 January 2014). When I find myself equating him with civilised values, I am aware of a mournful suspicion that 'the age demanded' and steered by very different standards of worth from those he embodied. Nor do I have in mind the rough and tumble of the poetry publishing and journalistic worlds alone, but also the superficially more rarefied environment of the academy. With unfailing fastidiousness, Dennis would address letters to me as 'Dr David Wheatley', a habit I attempted in vain to discourage. I worried that Dennis was excessively deferential to the academy – not a milieu, it must be said, exactly distinguished these days by a commitment to rising above the intellectual bottom line. A world in which a poet might become his 'research interest' was as unthinkable to Dennis as one in which being a poet meant going on Facebook to complain about a bad review you've just received. All the symptoms I am describing here, from the migration of poetry to the internet to the degradation of academic writing into 'outputs' for the Research Excellence Framework, have not come without a heavy price for the cultural ecosystem that produced and sustained Dennis's work. The shrinking of the world of small magazines where many of the pieces in *The Outnumbered Poet* first appeared, for instance, is an important factor in the future of the essay form, such as Dennis practised it. Where is a future Dennis to go?

One final memory. Justin Quinn has eloquently memorialised the lunchtime summits across the road from Dennis's office at which the three of us would do a round-the-houses on who was up, who was down, and who was down and out in Justin's and my youthful league tables, with Dennis acting as our benevolent ombudsman. Concerned, as I seem to remember, that the tip of his tie had blown backwards on the street on one such occasion, I silently restored it to, as I thought, its proper place. Also without a word, Dennis then re-draped it over his shoulder. While our conversations did not quite require the rolling up of sleeves, they were precision operations not to be disturbed by anything as untoward as a misplaced tie. This was, after all, the man who had written that misprints in poetry should occur with the same rarity that they occur in legislation. Proceedings concluded, Dennis would steal a glance at his fob-watch ('not an affectation') before we adjourned to the street outside for a brief coda, then revert to white rabbit mode, crossing the street and disappearing into the swallow hole of Castle House. Reascending to his eyrie over our heads, he was back in his domain, with a country waiting impatiently to be run. While the civil service will have contrived somehow or other to struggle along without him, I am much less confident of the republic of poetry's ability to continue in his absence.

Dennis O'Driscoll, *The Outnumbered Poet: Critical and Autobiographical Essays*. The Gallery Press, €17.50/€30. 472pp.

*Jane McKie*

## The Zephyr Aunts

There is an orchard where breezes
are aunts.
They fill the space between trees
with womanly scents,
offer themselves as chaperones
on this, the warmest day of the year.

Take them up on their offer –
they will be watchful
while fanning themselves. Zelda,
the one with the witch's name,
will sniff at a russet until she declares it
*totally unfit for human consumption.*

Marianne will ship her acquired
Spanish manners to the picnic,
clapping repeatedly at any zesty
remark, a dash of Catalonia
on the air – orange
and strong mountain fennel.

And Connie, who loved her husband
so fiercely, will be the first
to jump on the idea of marriage
when you test it aloud.
No timid chastisements
as you might expect of a zephyr,

but branches tormented –
a mini-cyclone around you,
picnic disrupted, memories
overturned. Ridiculous:
as if the world has room
for only one good marriage!

All three will sniff at your intended,
buffet the vigorous apple tree
you use to prop your back –
far too common, all fissured bark.
They fuss as you unscrew
another ripe globe from a branch.

This may not be what you want –
draughts at your wrist to freshen
your doubt. But they will be right.
You are too young. Before they died,
they knew enough between them
to live peaceably in the garden.

# Researching Livia's Garden Room for a School Project

It's odd, parlaying with a dead woman –
*strawberry tree, bay laurel, oleander*
Livia, Roman empress, whose famous
*Quercus ilex, Cornelian cherry*
garden graced an illusionistic room
*English oak, myrtle, hart's-tongue fern, early*
of four frescoed walls of foliage so
*dog violet, daisy, stinking chamomile*
bluish, fruit so golden, it makes us squint
*Italian cypress, stone pine, quince, opium*
with the desire to splice and grow our own
*poppy, cabbage rose, pomegranate, palm*
summers, especially in underpasses.

## Every Town Creates Its Saint

This town has blonde Saint Susan,
the skin between her fingers so cracked
that people joked it would grow
into webbing, her speech so hushed
that people tired of listening closely.
As a toddler, she was notably gentle,
her old-fashioned face turned always
to the sea. This continued for years
until she dropped out of college,
drove off in a Ford Cortina, friendless
mother to sand fleas, heading east
towards the cliffs and the cinematic
moment no one would witness.
Soon everyone observed her feast.

# The Specious Present

*[T]he short duration of which we are immediately and incessantly sensible.*
—William James

He'll never get to Myrtle Farm today,
he thinks. He woke up with the bloody shakes.

Not today, he thinks. The duvet's calling
as prickly and cloying as a thicket,
clock hands tremble on the same damn minute,
while the trees overhanging the stable roof
dangle burly limbs to drop in a storm
and he can't begin to lift the chainsaw.

Tomorrow, he thinks. He'll drive Long Furlong
willing the milometer to whizz round
those miles to where the A27
nuzzles the Downs and white slip roads lead to
Myrtle Farm and Myrtle Farm lies in state
like a lovely embalmed Eva Perón.

# from the place that isn't where I'm writing from

things grow and die
with predictable rhythm

three thin bird-peeps

green
green
      green

turn

grey
grey
      grey

all the light imprisoned
by the frames of the transparent engines
determining my view

## Our Last Night in a Small French Hotel

Before dawn I saw bones of birds
in the pendant shade; as first light
laid épées across the floor,
I spied shed feathers in your clothes.

I woke again when mid-morning
brought rain to my nostrils.
Windows wide, the air blue,
a high altitude silence to our room.

*Brian Hamill*

# Mr Summers

I was pulling a cage of frozen food when I thought I saw something happen. A woman standing at the hot beverages section. I dragged the cage into the pet food aisle so it wouldn't block peoples' way, then took something off the shelf. A packet of dried pig's ears. I went round into the next aisle as if I didn't know where to put it. The woman wasn't there. I walked on a bit further, and saw her looking about for a second, then moving her hand into one of the pockets in the big black anorak. She didn't see me. I stared in at the shelves for a second. I threw the pig's ears in among some tins, and walked away to the checkouts.

It was still early so the place was quiet. Donna and Paul were on the tills, just a couple of customers each. The supervisors' door was open and when I got nearer I could see Marion counting change out into the till on her desk. She heard me coming and peered over the tops of her glasses.

You better do the call, I said.

Aye?

Aye. Woman down at the deli.

What?

Meat and a jar of coffee.

You sure?

Aye.

Sure sure?

I seen her.

She lifted the phone from its holster on the wall and said, Mr Summers to the canteen please, Mr Summers to the canteen. The voice echoed in loud static through every room in the building. I stood outside the office and watched for who'd be coming first. It was a surprise when the door to the upstairs area opened, and Stevie and his assistant Jim stepped onto the shop floor.

That a security call wee man? Stevie said.

Aye. Woman in there somewhere with steak and coffee hidden in her jacket.

You positive?

Definitely, I said. Unless she's dropped it in the last couple of minutes.

She a junkie or what? the boss said.

I don't know.

Homeless?

Eh, I don't know.

I thought you seen her?

I did.

Look don't fuck about, Jim said. If you seen her you'd know. Does she look like a daft wee lassie trying to do some shoplifting, or does she look like a junkie?

Eh, she looks more like a junkie, I suppose. But she might not be. I dunno. I only seen her for a second.

Fine, Stevie said. Where the fuck's Pedro?

You want me to go find him? Jim asked.

Nah, if it's just one woman we should be OK. There's three of us eh.

You up for this wee man?

Eh, well, aye. Peter's in so he'll be here soon anyway.

Stevie laughed, He can deal wi her when he turns up then. But this is my shop, I'm not letting some fucking thief get anywhere near a door. Let's go.

You first, Jim said, poking me in the back. Find where she is then give us a signal.

A signal?

Aye, nod your head or something, whatever the fuck, just make it obvious.

Right, I said. I went back into the aisles. Donna was watching as I went past, going down by the soap powder and the bleach. I turned into the centre and saw Stevie and Jim creeping down after me. There was a special offer display of crisps, so I pretended to tidy it and glanced down at the deli. I started to think she'd got to one of the exits, but then she was there, right in the same aisle. She smiled at me. The jacket was zipped up to the neck, hands in the pockets. I smiled too, and went back round the corner. I didn't say anything, just pointed. Jim jogged down to guard the far end, the coins jingling away in his pockets. Stevie went the other way. The heels of his shoes clicked off the floor tiles, I saw in her face she knew it was too late to run.

Madam, have you got some of our merchandise in your coat there?
What? No.
Give the stuff to me now and leave, and we'll say nothing more about it.
I've not got anything.
Madam, we saw you on the cameras. Return the merchandise please.
I dunno what you're talking about. She nipped past him and walked towards the checkouts. Stevie went after her.
Madam, he said in a loud voice, I'll have to ask you to stop and open your coat.

She went straight through the checkout where Paul was sitting, pushing past a family with a full trolley.

Madam! Stevie shouted. She had a clear run at the door. Just as her hands were coming out of the pockets, Stevie reached out and grabbed the hood of the anorak. There was a crash. Glass and coffee granules were all round their feet. The woman twisted to free the hood. He kept his hold, and she hit him, reaching up and slashing her hand across his face. It was only when we saw the blood running down his cheek that Jim rushed her and grabbed the arm so it couldn't swing again. I moved forward not sure what to do. I was on her back with my arm round her neck when her legs gave way, and we fell. Something whacked me on the mouth and there was the taste of blood.

Grab her fucking ankles!
I threw myself on them and used my weight to stop them moving. She wriggled for about another minute.
Get off me! Get the fuck off!
Shut up, Stevie said down to her. Jim, check they pockets.
Jim felt around inside and the woman bucked, trying to get away from his hands. He brought out the packet of steak, a blue foam tray with cellophane over it, and dropped it on the floor.
That's not mine, the woman said. I never had that. That wasn't there.
I looked at Stevie's fat stubbled face. There was sweat on his forehead, blood trickling out from two scrapes on his cheek. It was sliding down his neck and forming a blob at the top of his collar.

Marion, Stevie shouted.

Aye, she said and she came toward us.

Phone the polis.

Naw! the woman said, and tried to fight her way out. I held onto the legs. Jim was whispering to Stevie but I couldn't make it out. I looked at the legs. Dirty grey trainers and wee whiteish socks with lace round the top. Her loose black trousers had rode up a bit, and her ankles were dainty white, wee buds of black hair sprouting through the dry-looking skin.

Och boys, a voice said. An old lady with two half-empty carrier bags was standing, watching. Yous shouldn't have to deal with that.

We're sorry for the disturbance, Jim said.

Don't be silly, the old woman said back. Is she one of they Romanians?

Am I fuck, the woman said.

You shut your mouth, Stevie said, giving her a shove back against the floor.

Ah! You can't fucking hurt me like that.

Terrible, the old woman said, shaking her head. Terrible what yous have to put up with. She wandered away.

Marion stuck her head out of her room and said, That's them phoned.

Fucking bastards!

The woman tried to heave Stevie off her chest. He smiled.

One unhappy punter we've got here eh Jim boy?

Aye, we'll no be asking her to fill out a questionnaire.

You fat fucking wanker, get the fuck off.

Keep your mouth shut please, Stevie said in a low voice, Tell it to the polis.

I looked along the checkouts, Paul and Donna were watching. So was Karen from the kiosk. Customers were staring, other ones just going about their business. Donna smiled and gave me a wee wave. The woman's body was rising and falling with every breath. Stevie panting quietly. The automatic doors were rolling open, rolling closed. The polis would get here soon. The floor felt cold. Jim had opened her jacket to see if she had any more jars or packets, and a slice of flabby white skin was visible between black sweatshirt and black trousers. It wobbled when she tried to move.

You're hurting me, she was saying.

Paul served an old couple, who turned and came right past us to leave out the side exit.

What's happened here? the old man said.

Shoplifting, Stevie said.

Oh, ya silly lassie.

I didn't do anything.

You're only making it worse, the old lady said. Carrying on like this. Look at ye.

Aye, Stevie nodded his head.

Aye, the husband agreed. There's something needing done, I know that much.

You're telling me, Jim said.

I couldn't see the woman's face anymore because of Stevie's ankle, but I thought I heard her gasping for a breath. What it must feel like to have three men on top of you, to be pinned down, not able to move your own arms and legs. What the shop must look like from so low down, turning sideways to see. I was near her feet, and our management team was hunkered over her chest and shoulders. The middle bit of her heaved slightly every now and then, and she was flexing her fingers. Her nail varnish was all chipped away, hardly any of it was left, just some wee red specks.

The couple kept looking down at her. Nobody spoke for a while. They wanted to wait and see what happened when the polis turned up, have a story to tell on the way home. I could hear the beeps of things being scanned through the tills. Eventually the old man said, Aye well, we're away up the road.

Bye now, said Jim.

Bye bye.

The two of them walked away slowly. I felt a laugh coming. I couldn't stop it. I put my head down and tried to focus on holding the woman's legs straight. Then I looked up at the ceiling. The security camera was turning slowly, scanning the floor. Stevie would have us all in his office to watch it later. We always did that when there'd been some action on the floor. A hand touched my shoulder and I jumped. It was old Mr Patel, one of the regulars.

Oh sorry son, sorry, I did not mean to startle you.

Eh, that's OK.

I was just wondering where you'd moved the Tennents to, you know the special offer stuff?

I glanced at Stevie.

I'm kind of busy here Mr Patel. I nodded down at the woman.

Yes yes that's fine son, you do what you have to do, but you tell me where it is, I will go find it myself.

It's been switched over to the other door sir, Stevie said, Near the butchery.

Oh right, I see, Mr Patel said, Thank you sir.

No bother at all.

He walked in between two checkouts and off in the direction of the meat chillers.

Bloody hell, I said.

I've never known a Hamilton Accie that was so into his lager, Jim said.

It's so he can punt it in his own shop, Stevie said. The fly bastard. He'll stick a fiver onto the price of every crate.

Where the fuck have you been? Jim shouted right in my ear.

I saw the baldy head of Peter, the security guard, coming in the kiosk door. He saw us, dropped his bag and ran over.

I was out on my break wasn't I.

Good timing, Stevie said. Look at my fucking face.

Jesus, Peter said. What happened? He looked down at the woman.

The wee man there, he spied her nicking stuff. So we asked her to put it back and she tried to do a runner.

Is that right?

No, the woman said. Is it fuck.

Stupid woman, Peter said. Cops phoned?

Aye, five minutes ago.

So she fought back did she?

She did aye, Stevie said. The polis'll be told the full story.

It's the smack, Peter said. Gives them fucking super-strength. You think they're going to be easy to take down, but you wouldn't believe how vicious they get. Took me ten minutes to restrain a junkie once. Just a wee fella he was, but he was mad wi the smack.

It was a struggle, Stevie said, We wereny expecting it, that was all.

The woman moaned. My arms, she said.

What was she stealing? Peter said.

You see that jar of coffee? Jim nodded at it.

Coffee? You're going to the slammer for some coffee granules? Ya daft cow. What, your man no in the mood for tea the day?

The three of them laughed, and the woman rolled her body suddenly and tipped us all to one side. She scrambled the other way, and she could've made it if it wasn't for the smashed jar. She slid on it and stumbled. Stevie flattened her again, and Peter and Jim got there too.

That's it, Stevie said. He was breathing heavy. Let's put her in the back office.

Sorry about this everybody, Marion was saying to the customers, The police will be here soon, never mind it.

Stevie had one arm and Jim got the other. Peter had his hand on the back of her neck. She was thrashing about but they got her through the door. I followed in. The corridor was empty.

You, Stevie said turning round, Stand by that door.

I went back and leaned against the frame.

You fucking bastards, she said, Fucking bastards.

Jim and Peter pulled her arms back. I noticed Stevie had wrapped his tie around his hand and then he hit her with it, clubbing his arm off the side of her head. I stepped right in front of the door so nobody could see in the glass panel.

The woman moved down into a sitting position.

So you can tell your junkie mates, Peter said, This is what you get if you try this shite in our fucking shop, alright? You understand?

I took a glance up and saw Stevie kneeling next to her.

She's alright, he said.

OK, I'll wait wi her in the office, Peter said, There'll be no more trouble.

Jim put his hand on my shoulder. Back to work fella, he said.

I went back through the door into the shop. Marion was nowhere to be seen. Paul and Donna were busy beeping through customers' items again. I waited for Jim to approach me. I wanted to be outside. The automatic door slid open and some fresh air came in. When my eyes opened Jim was there, shaking his head.

I'm away out to wait on the polis. If they ever get here that is. Too busy giving people fucking speeding tickets, never about when you need them eh.

I stood for another minute getting the breeze from the door. Then I remembered the cage I'd been pulling was all frozen stuff, and went back into the aisles to find it.

## David Harsent

### Fire: *love songs and descants*

So heap these on: letters, cuttings, poems, diaries, notebooks,
the black reports, the days of want and waste,
the double-entry records that set love alongside flaw,
everything said wrong, everything said in haste.

The pages curl; the words are borne up by the smoke…

                              *

'Come inside me noiseless, like snow on water; the ghost
  of yourself is all I want.'
                              <u>Notebook</u>: (*Malleus Maleficarum*) –
*Knowe that they kiss his ars the Father of Lyes
each lewd in hir tourne and comen therbye to gref.*

'I am lost in you. I know my name only when you speak it' –
this along with the rest, a fine burn, char and chaff. I stand backlit
against the blaze and featureless: proxy for the uninvited guest.

                              *

The way this winter sun slants through the branches to bed
down in the fire, taking light, giving light; the way smoke rolls
low across the garden and holds among fern and dogwood; the way
flame gathers faces from snapshots; the way it spoils,
in particular, my sight of you, yes, the way it spoils and sings.

*

Now it's quick shapes among trees, as if birds were flocking there,
grey birds and silent, flocking and lifting off. The singed leaves hiss.
the bole of the silver birch is tricked with soot. Time, perhaps, to confess,
though it might be just as well to settle for truth or dare
as seems to be the case in this double-portrait where someone
has come too close as if to smudge
the print, as if to darken it; and, though the moment has gone,
this remains: one soon to step back, the other close to the edge.

*

All this can be used or set aside: whatever arrives in sleep
or else is filched from memory: the Devil's patchwork
either way, a pattern of bafflement and sorrow, one slip
of the tongue, one half-hidden look, one whisky more or less.

There are standing shadows in the coming dark.

*

<u>Notebook</u>: (*Strindberg, To Damascus*): *When I'm alone
there's always someone else, although it's somehow myself.
I'm never myself alone. How can that be? The air thickens,
something takes shape. It can't be seen, but there it is beside me.*

\*

As if the moment will never quite pass
of shame and riddance, as if it might never seem strange…
A shovelling wind so the fire draws and drums.

'Nothing between us changes or can change.
If I were better suited to my dreams
love might have come more easily to me.'

\*

Your hand raised: *Not yet, not yet.* This was when the sea
rose above the sea-wall and swamped the quayside houses.
Another where you smile into the sun:
this was when it rained through the glare and rained again
on the drive inland, coming hard and slant, us in our usual disguises,
the world a blur and nothing said. Another where you turn
as if called, and this was when something broke
from the hedgerow, fast and frightened, barely seen
except: 'It had my eyes,' you said, meaning the fearful look
that now goes to the fire, shrivelled and lost.
<u>Notebook</u>:
*The Confessio – this will answer to sin without redemption
having no need of it: love-in-haste that will take
what it must and come to sorrow and then break clean.*

*

Frost in the air I breathe, leaf-fall under ice,
the evening star heavy and wet, clinker and ash
at the core, a ragged circle of scorch in the backyard grass.
'…nothing good can come of this or nothing
but good can come of this – which was it? I'm under glass.
I lie awake near-breathless: so still I can hear the sudden rush
as dawn comes in…'

'…last night a bird sang
out of darkness: unearthly, stark; I listened, lying still, so still,
as if I slept with knives…'

'…awake and near-breathless:
under glass as dawn comes in; my pulse might surge and stall…'

*

A crown of flame. The lattice shifts and drops. The letters soar
then settle, delicate and dark, all that's left of counterfeit and fear.

*

'… it's not only in dreams that I can go through fire…'

*Fran Brearton*

# Patterned silks and khaki scraps: Graves Redivivus

'My passport', says Robert Graves in his autobiography, *Good-bye to All That*, 'gives my nationality as "British subject"'. He goes on:

> Here I might parody Marcus Aurelius, who begins his Golden Book with the various ancestors and relations to whom he owes the virtues of a worthy Roman Emperor. Something of the sort about myself, and why I am not a Roman Emperor or even, except on occasions, an English gentleman. My mother's father's family, the von Ranke's, was a family of Saxon country pastors, not anciently noble. Leopold von Ranke, the first modern historian, my great-uncle, brought the 'von' into the family....Heinrich von Ranke, my grandfather...married, in London, my grandmother, a Schleswig-Dane [...] About the other side of my family. The Graves' have a pedigree that dates back to the Conquest, but is good as far as the reign of Henry VII. Colonel Graves, the regicide who was Ireton's chief of horse, is claimed as the founder of the Irish branch of the family. Limerick was its centre....My grandfather, on this side, was Protestant Bishop of Limerick....Of my father's mother, who was a Scotswoman, a Cheyne from Aberdeen, I have been able to get no information at all... The Cheyne pedigree was better than the Graves'; it was flawless right back to the medieval Scottish kings, to the two Balliols, the first and second Davids, and the Bruce.

Graves's obvious pride, however mischievous his tone may be, in this complicated German-Danish-Irish-Scottish heritage is also a delight in slipping the nets of expectation. For many readers, Graves is the quintessential Englishman – upper-class, public school and Oxbridge educated, a Captain in the Royal Welch Fusiliers (enlisting straight from the school's O.T.C.) – whose eccentricities serve only to confirm his self-assurance, the certainty of his 'place' in the world-order. And for many readers too, Graves is known in and through the texts, published relatively early in his career, which outsold anything else he ever wrote: the war memoir *Good-bye to All That* (1929), his biography of Lawrence of Arabia, *Lawrence and the Arabs* (1927), and – best-known of all perhaps, in consequence of their adaptation for BBC TV in the 1960s – the *Claudius* novels (1934).

Yet, as is often the case with Graves, the more detailed the information we are given, as we chase the beginning or end of the line ('I, Tiberius Claudius Drusus Nero Germanicus This-that-and-the-other…'), the more elusive he becomes. On the one hand there is the story of Graves the (English) prose writer, some of whose works are undisputed 'modern classics' in the literary canon, whose regimental loyalty remained undiminished despite his long and traumatic service in the trenches of the First World War, and who tried to serve his country again at the outbreak of World War II. On the other is the story of a man who wrote prose for the money (such as it was), who resolved early on 'never to make England my home again', and devoted his life to the service of the Muse. 'Since the age of fifteen', he tells us in *The White Goddess* (1948), 'poetry has been my ruling passion and I have never intentionally undertaken any task or formed any relationship that seemed inconsistent with poetic principles, which has sometimes won me the reputation of an eccentric'. Famous for his historical novels, he nonetheless declares himself to be free from history: as he writes in *The Common Asphodel* (1949), 'for the last twenty-two years [I] have abandoned the view that the poet is a public servant ministering to the caprices of a world in perpetual flux. I now regard him as independent of fashion and public service, a servant only of the true Muse, committed on her behalf to continuous personal variations on a single pre-historic, or post-historic, poetic theme; and have thus ceased to feel the frantic strain of swimming against the stream of time.' Shaped as he undoubtedly was by modern warfare, he deliberately opts out of a life 'geared to the industrial machine': 'I am nobody's servant and have chosen to live on the outskirts of a Majorcan mountain-village, Catholic but anti-ecclesiastical, where life is still ruled by the old agricultural cycle' (*The White Goddess,* 2nd ed. 1952).

Gravesian 'poetic principles', as manifest in the life and work, have not always met with approval. His professed devotion to his White (later Black) goddess ('mumbo-jumbo': Donald Davie); his speculations on tree alphabets ('interminable': Harold Bloom); his subservience to Laura Riding ('pussywhipped': Anthony Burgess), have all taken their toll on his reputation. So has his dismissive attitude, particularly in the 1955 Clark Lectures, towards other poets such as Yeats ('a new technique but nothing to say'); Pound (author of the 'sprawling, ignorant, indecent, unmelodious, seldom metrical *Cantos*, embellished with...illiterate Greek, Latin, Spanish, and Provencal snippets'); Eliot (who at least 'had once been, however briefly, a poet'); Auden (whose 'half-guinea...paid for Laura Riding's *Love as Love, Death as Death*, gave him no right to borrow half lines and whole lines from them for insertion in his own verse'), and Dylan Thomas ('He himself never pretended to be anything more than a young dog – witty, naughty, charming, irresponsible, and impenitent'). Philip Larkin is not the only English poet who struggles to reconcile Graves's mythopoeic world view and pronouncements on poetry with the kind of poetry Graves himself wrote. Nor has he been easy to 'place' in twentieth-century English poetry: proclaiming himself an outsider, the servant only of the Muse, he has not been easily conscripted for any of the groupings – from Modernism and the Thirties generation to the Movement and the 'new poetry' – through which the history of that poetry is so often told.

As if wilfully to compound the problem, Graves's reluctance to be pinned down extends beyond genealogy and geography to the ground of the text itself – which time and time again is taken from beneath the reader's feet. Over his sixty-year writing career, Graves published no fewer than eight *Collected Poems'*. In each new *Collected* he revised poems, often radically; and each *Collected* redefines the shape of Graves's past, by omitting poems (including most of his Great War poems) that he no longer considered part of his story. By the time his last *Collected Poems* appeared in 1975, only 189 of the 536 poems that appeared in books before 1959 made the final cut. The ever-shifting *oeuvre* generated by such extreme authorial decisions (which made some of his best-loved poems as hard to find as the vanishing point of his own origins) left readers, literally, at a loss. That situation was redressed in part by a *Selected Poems* edited by Paul O'Prey in 1986, and more fully, by the publication of a Penguin Classics edition of the *Complete Poems* (2003), edited by Beryl Graves and Dunstan Ward. The *Complete Poems* is a monumental achievement. But the sheer scale of the monument – over a thousand poems – is daunting; and almost a third of it comprises poems written from 1960-1975, the last years of his writing life, where Graves was over-prolific and at times over-determined, sometimes forgetting what he himself more clearly sees, in 'Dance of Words', as the need to 'start from lightening / And not forecast the rhythm…'

It is tempting to think of Graves, like Hardy or Whitman before him, as *sui generis*, as the outsider who is at once everywhere and nowhere, finding a 'home' in Majorca if never quite 'at home' in the English poetic tradition. But he is not without obvious poetic affinities, however much they may have been lost to sight in recent decades. W.H. Auden's famous elegy for Yeats described the elder poet as 'silly like us', yet whose 'gift survived it all'. The 'silliness' – Yeats's *Vision* dictated to his wife by spirits; his belief in magic; his occult practices – is in evidence in a different way in Graves too: oghams not the occult, magic mushrooms if not magic *per se*, goddesses rather than gyres. So too is the poetic 'gift' that survives it all. If it is not 'mad Ireland' that hurts Graves into poetry, the complex politics of identity, thrown into sharp relief by the 'silly / Mad War', as he calls it in 'Over the Brazier', in which he fought, hurt him into the creation of an extra-poetic apparatus, and into the living of an extraordinary life, in order to preserve and enable the 'ruling passion' of poetry. The links between Graves and his most immediate precursor, links that he would always strongly deny, are sometimes so obvious, indeed, as to make his denials a perverse form of affirmation. Yeats and Graves are also twin poles of influence for a later generation of Irish poets, who encountered Graves's work in the 1950s, when his poetic powers were at their height, and when the body of work he had produced up to that point contained some of the outstanding poems of the century: 'Mid-Winter Waking', 'To Juan at the Winter Solstice', 'Counting the Beats', 'The White Goddess'.

It's fitting, therefore, that Graves, who sometimes did himself few favours, should now be re-presented to a contemporary audience; and by one of his immediate 'descendents' in Ireland, Michael Longley. Longley's superb new edition of Graves's *Selected Poems* (2013) is welcome on several fronts: first, in its skilful distillation from a massive *oeuvre* of an intelligible Graves whose poetic brilliance is in evidence on every page of the book; second, in its recovery of the war poems suppressed by Graves, those 'khaki scraps' without which the Gravesian story is incomplete. Third, and more obliquely perhaps, the selection reminds us both of Graves's Irish heritage and, more importantly, of his legacy in Ireland, as a poet and critic profoundly influential – in diverse ways – on the work of Montague, Longley, Heaney, and Mahon, as well as on that of Paul Muldoon or Peter McDonald. Graves is not here 'recovered' for Ireland in the manner of MacNeice – whose reputation, as Mahon put it, came 'to rest' in his birthplace, the North of Ireland, in the 1970s. Graves, who delighted that his father 'broke the geographical connexion with Ireland' before he was born, sits uneasily as an 'Irish poet', and John Montague's inclusion of Graves in the *Faber Book of Irish Verse* (1974) was not uncontroversial. Writing to Graves in March 1974, Montague observes that 'My Irish anthology has risen an English hare. I will endeavour to tweak his tail a little on your behalf, by reminding him of your ancestry and many statements on the subject…'. Later the same year, Montague tells him: 'I had a great time defending your Irishness against ignorant reviewers who seem to have such set views'.

Nevertheless, whilst Graves may have been less concerned to affirm his 'Irishness' than Montague (he does so at school, under pressure from his peers about his German side in the context of a pre-War spirit of Entente Cordiale, and occasionally thereafter when claiming particular insights into other Irish writers, or Celtic scholarship), the foreword to Graves's *Collected Poems* 1959 does contain within it an explicit claim about his 'poetic tradition' that he makes nowhere else:

> These poems follow a roughly chronological order. The first was written in the summer of 1914, and shows where I stood at the age of nineteen before getting caught up by the First World War, which permanently changed my outlook on life.
>
> Sixteen years of the forty-five that have since elapsed were spent in England; nineteen in Spain – which has become my permanent home – most of the rest in Wales, France, Egypt, Switzerland and the United States. But somehow these poems have never adopted a foreign accent or colouring; they remain true to the Anglo-Irish poetic tradition into which I was born.

It is that sense of a shared tradition that informs the relationship between Montague and Graves, and Montague helped to organise Graves's only poetry readings in Ireland, in 1975. For Longley, as for Mahon, it is this 1959 *Collected Poems* which made Graves 'one of our heroes'. In the introduction to his Graves *Selected*, he describes how he and Mahon 'read his poems aloud to each other, counting the beats with our hands…' whilst both undergraduates at Trinity. 'As a master of the singing line, complex syntax and stanzaic patterns', he goes on to say, 'Graves was an ideal focus for two apprentices.' Early poems published in the student magazine *Icarus* evidence a Gravesian, as well as Yeatsian haunting, as in Mahon's 'Whatever Fall or Blow' (with its echoes of 'To Juan at the Winter Solstice' and 'The White Goddess', as well as Yeats's 'The Song of the Happy Shepherd') from March 1961:

> The uncertainty of words
> Spoken alone, the quaint
> Coinage of looks that bridge
> No chaos, invoke no saint,
> Of two who, worlds apart,
> Came so without complaint.

An early essay in *Icarus* (March 1962) by Edna Longley – then Edna Broderick and also an undergraduate at Trinity – gives some indication of the critical climate in which she, Longley, and Mahon were discovering and appreciating Graves. Too often, she complains, 'poetry comes a poor second to poetics, philosophy, sensation, self-pity, literature, or superficial aspects of the modern world. There is a frequent misunderstanding as to what is powerful and modern in poetry, a tendency to be moved by shock tactics of statement and description. Good poetry never shocks – it chills or warms. Four of the most powerful lines in modern poetry occur in a poem by Robert Graves about Christmas trees:

> But he knew better, did the Christmas robin –
> The murderous robin with his breast aglow
> And legs apart, in a spade-handle perched:
> He prophesied more snow, and worse than snow.'

The comments are a slightly more restrained version of the effect, or the 'strange feeling' generated by poetry as outlined by Graves himself in

*The White Goddess*. A.E. Housman's test of a true poem', he tells us, 'was simple and practical: does it make the hairs of one's chin bristle if one repeats it silently while shaving?' (It's a male-only beardless test.) The difficulty in achieving the surface simplicity that nevertheless has the capacity to 'chill or warm', or as Graves has it to generate both 'delight and horror', is evident in Mahon's juvenilia. A Gravesian ambition informs 'O Where Now is Robin' *(Icarus*, 1961) albeit not fully realised at this stage:

> O where now is Robin, the snowman I made
> With my own hands, with my own hands?
> ...
> O who killed Cock Robin, so red and white?
> The killer bird rose with flaming glands
>
> In the dead of night, in the dead of night,
> And tore him apart with your own hands,
>
> With your own hands.

Graves was in the air in Belfast as well as Dublin in the early 1960s. In *Stepping Stones*, recalling his courtship of Marie, Seamus Heaney notes that 'At St Mary's College, Marie had done extended essays on Louis MacNeice and Robert Graves; this meant that, from the start, poetry was one of the elements in the mix. So there was a muse energy in the air all right. "The wood astir", as Graves says. A call to separateness, to some sort of extravagance, to be more yourself'. He alludes here to the final stanza of Graves's 'The White Goddess':

> Green sap of Spring in the young wood a-stir
> Will celebrate the Mountain Mother,
> And every song-bird shout awhile for her;
> But we are gifted, even in November
> Rawest of seasons, with so huge a sense
> Of her nakedly worn magnificence
> We forget cruelty and past betrayal,
> Heedless of where the next bright bolt may fall.

'The wood astir' also evokes an early unpublished war poem ('The Survivor Comes Home'), written, he tells us, 'when I had the horrors', that as yet lacks the mythological compensation for suffering:

> What stirs in the drenching wood?
> What drags at my heart, my feet?
> What stirs in the wood?
>
> Nothing stirs, nothing cries.

But it is the post-1945 Graves of goddess-worship, with the cyclical pattern of sacrificial death and rebirth enshrined in his mythological thinking, who speaks most immediately to Heaney in the 1960s – more than the Graves of 'complex syntax and stanzaic patterns', or, indeed, of a sometimes metaphysical bleakness that calls to Mahon's imagination. ('Extravagance' is present in Graves's ideas and his prose writings, but seldom in his poetry.) Heaney's early criticism, more so than his poetry, is packed with Gravesian borrowings – from the 'cults and devotees of a god and goddess' and the play of masculine against feminine, to his early observations on the nature of inspiration. The influence of Graves is deep-rooted and long-lasting: almost four decades later, as he tells us in *Stepping Stones*, Heaney lectured at Harvard on both Graves and Horace as poets 'writing about transformation caused by the "bright bolt" of terror', finding, after 9/11, that the 'shock-and-awe factor…matched what I and everybody else was feeling'.

The Gravesian legacy in Ireland is as complex and contradictory as the man himself. As a love poet, the influence of poems such as 'Mid-Winter Waking', 'Counting the Beats' or 'She Tells Her Love While Half Asleep', those flawless lyrics of Graves's middle years, is evident in Montague's 'All Legendary Obstacles', Mahon's 'Preface to a Love Poem', Longley's 'Epithalamion', or Heaney's 'Poem: *for Marie*'. But the technically accomplished muse-poetry is only one element in an infinitely various and war-haunted *oeuvre*. Longley opens his *Selected* Graves with a little-known (uncollected) poem, 'The Patchwork Quilt', included in a letter to Sassoon in July 1918:

> Here is this patchwork quilt I've made

> Of patterned silks and old brocade,
> Small faded rags in memory rich
> Sewn each to each in feather stitch,
> But if you stare aghast perhaps
> At certain muddied khaki scraps
> Or trophy-fragments of field grey,
> Clotted and torn, a grim display
> That never decked white sheets before,
> Blame my dazed head, blame bloody war.

Longley's own poetry is littered with khaki scraps too – the memories passed on by his father, a veteran of the First World War. And the 'patchwork' of this poem puts the two poets in dialogue in a way which is almost uncanny: Longley, before encountering this poem in 2012, had, more than a decade earlier, stitched his own poems into the quilt of *The Weather in Japan* (2000): 'Sometimes the quilts were white for weddings, the design / Made up of stitches and the shadows cast by stitches. / And the quilts for funerals? How do you sew the night?' ('The Design'). In *The White Goddess* Graves argues that 'it is not too much to say that all original discoveries and inventions and musical and poetic compositions are the result of proleptic thought – the anticipation, by means of a suspension of time, of a result that could not have been arrived at by inductive reasoning – and of what may be called analeptic thought, the recovery of lost events by the same suspension'. It is appropriate enough, therefore, that the later poet is written into the fabric of Graves's own poetry, as Graves himself, dazed by 'bloody war', nevertheless survives to be written by his 'heirs' into the tapestry of Irish literary history.

*Miriam Gamble*

## Personification

On the ferry to Larne, someone shouts 'That cunt of a curtain!'
and you're back where inanimate objects have malicious intent;
where soft furnishings are mischievous,
looking for trouble, and white goods present a staunch, rebellious mien
when, in levering them into the perfect slot, your da… encounters problems.

In the soft-pile carpet is the spirit of an elf
who wants to be out in the woods changing workmen to donkey kings;
the stereo, if it could, would seize, or sign itself away for scrap.
As for the old cloth deckchairs, summer nights to the tune of the midge
they rustle their foliage, flex their ancient wooden jaws like traps.

# The Brutality of Koala Song

Hairy little don
with the voice of a sex-starved maniac,
your foot hanging out of the gum,
when pressed, should deliver a note
of Augustan sweetness;

it ought to be that you digress,
with well-meaning absent-minded intent,
on subjects of a day
that is thoroughly outdated;
you ought to sport
spectacles and a powdered wig.

You balance your bum
on the meanest twig
and sleep all day –
a twig that shouldn't hold you,
your bulbous weight;
your curled ball is ridiculous
to the sight.

    Who
tutored you in this rapist's language,
little clerk, little Dickensian notary,
this bass guttural
that rocks the forest canopy
and that keeps me awake all night?

Gorillas will deface each other.
But you —
you have snuff in your ears,
you chew your poppies.
You're a natural non-sequitur.
Honest the hand
that chose to paint you grey,
with just occasional daubs
of black and white.

# Pirate Music

For ten plus years
they monitor the call,
deepening and desperate,
off range,
of a whale
believed to be
the only one
of its kind

no other marks
his particular rhythms;
with timbre
and timing out of sync
he is doomed
to understand
and not
to be understood

in waters
darker than
the devil's blood
he exists,
porous and piratical,
his temperament
which once was good
soured from
the endless lonely nights
and vacant days

(o fish
softly skinned,
o mammal)

where he sings,
adamant, tremolo,
of works not
shown to man

turn the dial;
he is in
your neighbourhood
and this is not
a parable

## An Encounter

I spied the kitten on the road
in the country outside Dundalk,
thought to take it home with me.
This my first reckoning with a feral cat.

It bit, spat, even mustered a fart
from the reaches of its armoury.
I loosed it in a nettle patch
and went upon my way, whereat
the hissing slowly dimmed and died.

And there, on the uncontroverted throne
of its scalding freedom,
the little fucker sat, alone,
a snicker tall and a hiccup wide,
one single snarling animated burr.

Sun drenched the ears with glory;
dew glittered on the risen back like pride.

# According to the Dalai Lama

Out of a random list of animals
I place horse above tiger
and both ahead of sheep,
thus scuppering my credentials as a wife.

My personality is smelly (dog),
while yours, true to form, is furry like a cat.
Our sex, kin to coffee, is fragrant;
the rat, my enemy, is stigmatised.

A consolation prize of the wish
made at the outset will happen if, by Saturday,
I forward this to $x$ number of friends
one of whom should be my soul mate (white).

Red, yellow and green
are also not to be forgotten.
As for the sea (death), that's my view of life.

*Regi Claire*

# Five Dances for Topaz

Topaz felt glowing inside. Holding a bunch of daffodils, she dance-stepped into the room, light and feathery on her feet despite her weight, and said, 'Good morning, Mr Jardine.' She still called him that and always would.

The old man glanced up as she approached, his magnifying glass hovering close above the newspaper on the table. 'My dear girl,' he replied.

Ever since Mrs Jardine had died, his vocabulary had shrunk. Topaz reckoned he was losing about a dozen words a day. All his favourite obscure expressions had vanished from his conversation, if 'conversation' it could be termed. No more 'crepuscular', 'obfuscation' or 'unequivocal', just plain English, which, to be honest, suited her fine. Even his French hardly amounted to more now than a 'bonne nuit', 'bon appétit' or, his favourite with a pre-lunch beer, 'santé!'

Yet he kept treating her – really quite obstinately, she felt – like a child. But that would change soon now, very soon. Topaz touched her belly, smiling to herself. Only look at him, hunched in his heather-grey tweed jacket with the chocolate stains on both lapels. Look at his white hair like an untrimmed hedge – had his comb gone walkabout, too? Those tall tales that had made him famous in the past had worn as thin as the seashell he was inspecting and –

Seashell? Yes, lying on top of the *Evening News*.

The old man had lifted the shell to his ear and seemed to be listening to it. He blinked at her. Nothing to hear, of course. Topaz shook her head and slowly, almost reluctantly, he set the shell back down on the table. A pigeon, yes, that's what he reminded her of – an ancient pigeon, windblown, dusty, abandoned by the flock. But now Mr Jardine's eyes suddenly lit up. 'Oh, it's you, Topaz. For a moment I thought that Mrs Jar…' He broke off and Topaz noticed his hands were shaking.

She moved closer, placing the flowers on the table. 'Where did you get that seashell, Mr Jardine? May I see it?'

He nodded and slid it towards her.

The shell was a creamy, near-translucent pink, with a minute fissure, barely visible, in its lustrous inside of mother-of-pearl. 'It's lovely...' Topaz paused and ran a finger around the rim, pressing hard enough to feel the sharp edge graze her skin. 'A gift from one of the other residents?'

Mr Jardine gave her a confused look and she quickly passed the shell back to him. She nodded towards the daffodils, 'I'll just put these in a vase and then I'll make us a cup of tea, shall I? To get the day started in style.'

'That would be nice, dear. Thank you.' He sounded relieved.

Topaz was about to turn away and pirouette through the archway leading into the kitchen when Mr Jardine hauled himself upright in his chair.

Next moment there came the unmistakable squeak-and-squeal of little Charlie's voice – she remembered it quite clearly from watching the show on Blue Peter as a goggle-eyed kid: 'And a chocolate biscuit for me. No, make that two. I need to line my nonexistent stomach.'

The laugh that followed was so loud it startled her. 'Nonexistent' was no longer a word Mr Jardine used. And little Charlie was long gone. Mrs Jardine had thrown him out when her husband reached pension age. 'Too shabby after all that touring, and his head keeps falling off,' she had told Topaz. Topaz's reply that she'd be happy to make him a new head and find him a new outfit had been met with silence. From then on, Mr Jardine had sat in his armchair by the gas fire, snoring his afternoons away in the stuffiness of the too-hot lounge while Mrs Jardine had taken his agent's phone calls in the bedroom until they became fewer and farther in between, and finally stopped altogether.

Topaz had tried to sympathise with the woman. Having a famous husband and being generally referred to as 'Mr Jardine's wife' must have been galling. Soul-destroying, really. No doubt this had hastened the old lady's decline and brought on her death the previous summer.

As she waited for the kettle to cool down, Topaz stood gazing at the daffodils splayed out in the glass vase with the frilly neck. Soon the warmth would make them burst from their papery sheaths; she could almost hear their secret rustlings as they readied themselves, drawing strength from the water. She covered her belly with both hands and pressed gently, then harder, until she was sure she could feel a shifting, somersaulting lurch. Her baby boy – because it would have to be a boy, wouldn't it? – was gearing up for some serious kicking. One day, she knew, he would play for the national team. How proud she would be then – how very proud.

Light and feathery on her feet despite her weight, Topaz dance-stepped along the hallway, bearing a bunch of red tulips from her hidden garden.

'Good morning, Mr Jardine,' she called out.

And there he was in his bedroom, seated in the off-white rattan chair with a sock in one hand, trying in vain to tug it over his left foot. His toenails needed cut, she noted automatically, wondering if the bathroom scissors were still in the mirror cabinet above the sink before remembering that Mrs Jardine had got rid of them and instead bought nail clippers, a nostril-hair trimmer and individually wrapped sticking plasters.

'The seashell,' he cried. 'Where, where, where is my seashell?' His voice had risen to a querulous, plaintive pitch.

'Don't you worry.' Laying the tulips on one of Mrs Jardine's hand-crocheted doilies on the chest of drawers, Topaz reached for the sock and slipped it over his foot; no time now to fuss with the clippers, upsetting the old man still further. Already his eyes had begun to tear over with a viscous film that refused to spill, making them look like blurry mirrors.

'Slippers,' she ordered. Then, 'Come on now, Mr Jardine, cheer up. We'll play a game of cards.' A coaxer of old men, her friends called her.

Game over – Topaz had lost as usual, deliberately – she was sitting enjoying a mid-morning ginger and chocolate biscuit when there was a rap at the door.

'Hello? Anybody home? Wait till you see this, Mr Jardine. Genuine new stock.' It was salesman Todd. Again.

Before she could stop the old man, he had opened the door and in strode Todd with his carcass of a leather suitcase. 'Hi there,' he said breezily.

In the bright sunlight streaming through the window Topaz could see the stubble on his skin. The gold tooth in the corner of his mouth seemed to wink at her. She quickly swallowed the rest of her biscuit and jumped out of her seat, grabbing a duster and flicking it over the bookshelf with the Mills and Boon paperbacks that had entertained Mrs Jardine while her husband was on tour. Wiping down the wooden mantelpiece she had polished only the other day, she noticed a faint scratch mark near the clock, where the seashell had been.

Frankly, she was not surprised at its loss. Every so often things disappeared in the little flat. Small things, hardly noticeable. As her colleague Roanna frequently pointed out, Mr Jardine *was* getting forgetful. Truth be told, she was surprised that not more stuff had gone missing, considering all the people with access to the place: the building's caretaker couple, the newspaper boy, the laundry man, the barber, the window cleaner, the occasional plumber trying yet again to fix the leaking bathroom tap, the doctor, the prescription delivery girl, and that salesman…

Topaz glanced over at Todd, whose sample case lay spilling its insides right next to Mr Jardine's chair. Two heads, one grey, one white, both going bald, were bent over the contents. She sighed when she saw Todd offload yet another tin of Brodie's shortbread 'just for starters'. By the time Mr Jardine was invited to 'feel the softness' of half a dozen cheaply flabby, garish green tea towels, 'a bargain at only one pound fifty each, plus green is soothing to the eyes after an evening of TV', she had heard plenty.

'Mr Jardine has enough merchandise to open his own shop, Mr Todd – as you well know…' Pulling the bundle out of the salesman's hands, she brought it up to her face, then wrinkled her nose. 'Thought so: mothballed since the last century.' And she stuffed the lot back into the case.

'Oh, but I want one of these for a pillow because my head keeps falling off,' a pip-squeaky voice suddenly announced beside her.

Todd laughed out loud and clapped his applause.

Topaz turned away. The shower needed cleaning quite urgently, she had just remembered. The door shut behind her with a satisfying bang.

Salesman Todd departed nearly an hour later – an hour that Topaz spent cooped up in the bathroom, sweating herself into a frenzy as she heard the word 'mothballed' echo all around her while she slapped the sponge (one of Todd's) first round the shower, then the sink, squeezing and wringing it extra hard, then scrubbing the toilet with, yes, a brush from Todd, scrubbing so hard the handle broke and the brush fell into the bowl, by which time she was swearing freely and loudly, apologising (in whispers) only to the baby she imagined she could feel sloshing about inside herself.

Feathery light on her feet despite her weight, Topaz dance-stepped into the flat, a pale pink shell (one of her own) clasped in her hand.

'Hello, Mr Jardine!'

'Bonjour, mademoiselle,' came his reply from behind the bathroom door, which was standing ajar. One of the old man's better days, it seemed.

Topaz could hear him urinating noisily into the toilet bowl as she took off her shoes and put on the plastic clogs reserved for her clients – easier to clean if there was an 'accident'. Averting her eyes, she went quickly into the lounge to set her shell on the mantelpiece. It wasn't perhaps as delicate as its predecessor but similar enough to fool the untrained eye. Just in case, she stuffed Mr Jardine's magnifying glass down the back of the constipated-looking armchair in the corner. Formerly Mrs Jardine's, the chair was no longer used, except for certain individuals like the health-and-safety person or the new doctor who thought he knew it all, though, Topaz was sure, he would be incapable of locating the fog lights on his own BMW. She was thumping the embroidered cushion back into position when a shriek of beeps alerted her to 'please replace the handset and try again please replace the handset and…' The old man must have hidden the phone to avoid having to deal with 'the world' – old neighbours and acquaintances, mainly.

'No,' shouted a voice from the receiver, 'I can't find it anywhere. Shut up now I'm…'

Then a whisper, perhaps the whisper of a child. 'Please,' it said, 'can you help me, whoever you are? He's unscrewed the light bulb and…'

'…replace the handset and try again please replace…' the automated message cut in.

Crossed wires even in this digital age? Topaz shook her head as she returned the phone to its base on the antique tallboy.

Anyway, it was showtime or, rather, shower time. Not a time either she or Mr Jardine relished. On her first day with him, the old man had insisted on wearing his faded red swimming trunks. But when the water began sluicing down his body, they had flopped right off his spindly haunches and had lain twisting and flailing between his submerged feet like something fleshily alive, and drowning.

Topaz flinched at the memory. Then she hugged herself, stroked her belly, which felt drum-skin tight and round. 'Sleep, little boy,' she breathed into herself, 'sleepy-sleep. Don't take any notice of your mummy's fancies.'

Carrying a bouquet of white roses from an obliging bush along the way, Topaz dance-stepped into a sunny patch on the hall floor, light and feathery on her feet despite her weight.

'Good morning, Mr Jardine!'

Mr Jardine made no answer. He either hadn't put his hearing aids in or was still in bed – how could he, on a bright, fresh morning like this?

Topaz went into the lounge where the curtains had been opened. On top of yesterday's *Evening News*, splotch-bang in the middle of a fat-faced politician, sat the ceramic tea bag tray, a relic of Mrs Jardine's pottery-collecting days. And, nestling against a dripping tea bag, were the brittle remains of two seashells. So he had *not* lost his, after all. But it was broken now, split along the fault line of that old fissure, split like a pod spilling its seed. Not that there was any seed. Nothing apart from a few stray tea grains that had leaked from a hole in the bag.

In the kitchen, a plate with a half-eaten slice of toast sat next to a sticky jar of marmalade and a half-drunk mug of tea. Sulking in the bedroom, was he?

But Mr Jardine was not in the bedroom.

Topaz found him behind the shower curtain, slumped on the blue IKEA plastic stool she had bought him for his last birthday, so he would feel less exposed while getting his privates washed. He was still in his pyjamas. And he was crying, head hung low like an overripe fruit on a too-thin stalk. At least thirty minutes' worth of tears, Topaz couldn't help thinking – the professional part of her brain had registered the dribbles of spit on his front and the soaked state of his right sleeve, which he used like a windscreen wiper, at regular intervals.

'My goodness, Mr Jardine, what's wrong?' Sometimes, feigning ignorance was the safest option.

At first he pushed her away. Wouldn't even look up. Just dropped his head lower, in danger of falling fully off, like that of little Charlie.

'I saw her again last night,' he mumbled finally, in between gulps. 'She was holding out the seashell. The seashell she had given me on our honeymoon in Nice... *Nice*,' he repeated, with another sob, 'lovely, lovely Nice!' Then, all at once, he sat up straight; his head seemed to snap back into place, realigning itself with his spine. His eyes lost their customary fuzziness.

'The bloody seashell she had fobbed him off with instead of a child,' came little Charlie's squeak-and-squeal. 'And now the seashells are multiplying. Bloody bitch!'

Topaz tried not to look shocked, or concerned. If she ignored Charlie, the voice usually quietened down again pretty quick. 'Like pressing the hibernate button,' she joked to her friends sometimes. 'Wish I could delete him altogether!'

Now and again, Mr Jardine had complained of hearing his wife's footsteps in the night; she would creep up to his bed, he said, and touch the bedclothes, not to tuck him in but to pull off the blanket, toss it to the floor – as if she was looking for someone. Someone small and burrowing.

Later, after Topaz had cleared away the breakfast things, including the two broken seashells, they played a game of Patience. Still later, when Mr Jardine was settled at the table with a bottle of pre-lunch beer – 'santé!' she had said to him - and his freshly delivered paper, grumbling about his missing magnifying glass, Topaz brought out her bag of wool. Because, yes, she had taken up knitting again.

And what a pleasure it was! Knitting and moving her hands just so. Creating something from a small ball of wool uncoiling at her feet and the yarn snaking around her fingers, pulling tight, tight, tight, and the needles *click-click*ing with the sound of so many tiny knives being sharpened, endlessly. Between their silvery grey flashes the fabric grew in a soft dangle. Longer and longer it grew until it flopped onto her belly, her thighs. What was she knitting, she wondered at one point, once the sheer pleasure of creation had abated a little and given way to sudden weariness.

'What am I knitting?' she addressed Mr Jardine, tentatively almost.

He looked up from his *Evening News* and replied without thinking, 'Why, you are making a puppet, of course. Can't you see?'

And he was right: there between her legs was what looked like half the body of a figure, complete with head, torso, arms and leg stumps, not quite finished yet.

*Topaz*, she heard an inner voice say, warningly. And the implication was plain. Topaz had never been a particularly gifted knitter before. At school, in handicraft, she had always had help from her best friend, a champion knitter who took part in competitions, knitting whole shawls within less than a day, her fingers moving like the pistons of a machine, so mechanically it had scared Topaz. In secret she had wondered if her friend had inherited, due perhaps to some weird genetic modification, the genes from a spider. After all, she had heard that there were tomatoes with pig genes, so why not humans with genes from mushrooms, for example, or indeed, spiders?

Topaz patted her belly. She pictured her little boy beginning to unfold and stretch himself in the dark, unfurling his perfect fingers one by one as if they were petals, then his toes, readying himself to burst free.

Topaz felt glowing outside. Carrying a bunch of dahlias, juicy pink and tinted with gold like tiny baby faces, she dance-stepped into the room, light and feathery on her feet, her weight all gone now.

'Good morning, Mr Jardine.' She greeted him with a smile.

The old man glanced up as she approached, his magnifying glass, which had magically reappeared one morning, hovering close above his paper.

'My dear girl,' he said.

Topaz gave him another smile before she went into the kitchen to place the dahlias in the frilly-necked vase. She smelt them for a moment, inhaling their sappy warm scent, then she kissed them, very gently, and carried them back into the lounge, positioning them well out of the range of Mr Jardine's rustling newspaper.

Having put the bedroom to rights, even whipping the hoover out of the cupboard for a cursory clean, she suggested a cup of tea. The tea was bait because, first of all, Mr Jardine's hair needed washed (the home-visit barber was on holiday), and he hated getting wet at the best of times. His shower wasn't due until the end of the week. Roanna's turn, thankfully. Topaz fetched the orange plastic basin and a stack of Mr Jardine's new towels. The old man's hair had grown so thin by now that a bit of sponging would do the trick. The less fuss the better.

It was afterwards that she heard a small voice calling, 'Topaz! Topaz! Topaz!' The voice was whispery low and seemed to wax and wane, as if coming to her from a great distance, across mountains and forests and snowy wastes patrolled by hungry, red-eyed wolves, across the seven seas. Well, perhaps not quite, she reminded herself. After all, she wasn't living in a fairytale. She was a denizen of the twenty-first century engaged at present in making a cup of tea for herself and her octogenarian client in his well-appointed kitchen that boasted not just a microwave, but a glass-ceramic hob and a new-fangled kettle that boiled only the amount of water you needed, to save energy. A talking kettle, in fact; it spoke in a horrible piping voice which seemed to work well with those hard of hearing, especially the elderly. 'I am thirsty,' it would say, 'please fill me up.' Or, inanely, 'One cup is for one,' 'Two cups is for company,' 'Three cups is a gathering.'

The first time Topaz had jumped nearly out of her skin and looked around. But Mr Jardine had been asleep in his chair by the window, snoring and grunting. The only thing that had moved was a wisp of white hair next to his open mouth.

Again that new voice came, sounding louder now, 'Topaz! Topaz!', more insistent. 'I want to play with you. Please play with me, Topaz. Come and dance with me.'

Topaz lifted her head and looked out the window. Above the ancient linden tree in the parking lot, the sky was a sugar-dust blue. The vapour trails of two airplanes seemed set at quarter past ten.

Well, why not? she thought. Why not dance for just a little while? She felt her heart skip a beat, as if in anticipation.

# Ricardo Pau-Llosa

## Four Horsemen Man

A friend came over with tickets
to a basketball game of great importance
except the man loathes sports so he called
up other friends, so the damn tickets
wouldn't go to waste, imagined frantic lines
of bowed heads waiting to be scalped,
and here he had these two keys
to everyone's paradise but his own,
and one after the other said they would have
loved to go but so little notice, made plans
with kids already, and the wife,
and next time tell me sooner,
but he didn't know he was going to have
these wondrous little pieces of cardboard
everyone was supposed to lust for
yet no one did. He looked at them
in the trash, little bent boomerangs
trapped between bacon plastic and eggshells.
The man thought, How like fear desire is –
no one plans to run from a fire
but does anyway.

# Tower of Babel Man

The man had a glazed job, firmly bureaucratic,
but his two friends were part of a massive layoff
so he took them to the Indian casino outside town,

where they blew their last superfluous income
on this and that, machines, umbrella drinks,
big tits. And the man thought what he'd do

if suddenly the language of his life changed,
the checkbook did not roll in biweekly as it had
done for 24 years, and the cracks in the structure

of the world became accusatory fingers pointed
at him. I'd change everything, the man pondered
to himself. Start wearing brighter colors, go on a diet,

walk the dog two and even three times a day,
do his laundry at night so the dryer hum
would lull him to sleep, read Lear and listen

to classical stations since love lyrics would tear at him
the way they've done since his wife betrayed him.
But he had lost nothing, so why worry?

# Spirit Man

Was the laundry tumble of dream
due to the content, the meaning thereof,
or the toxic fumes he inhaled as a boy?

Havana, 1959. Miramar —
new professional-class
apartment building by the sea.

Jeeps drive around before sunset
pouring white clouds of insecticide
to kill the mosquitoes.

Cubans are proud of Carlos Finlay,
say Walter Reed stole his glory.
We found the culprit to malaria

and yellow fever. Years later,
dengue would be the star.
Now the neighborhood kids run

after the jeep spouting the white
drifts that ingest the houses, lick
the polished cars, dress the palms.

The fog ballets on terraces, competes
with clouds catching the last lights
of day against a tropic sky that paints itself

garishly to no avail, because we're in love
with the thickness that barrels out of the back
of a clattering shadow. Children run after the spirit

breathless, planning the dream's
closing arguments. Only their laughter
can wake up the jury.

*Colin Graham*

# The Directive

*The Mass Observation movement was founded in 1937 by Charles Madge, Tom Harrisson and Humphrey Jennings. Its aim was to understand everyday life in Britain and its methods included first-hand (and, often, undercover) observation of working-class activities. It also solicited diaries from willing participants, and sent out lists of questions, to be completed by volunteers who had signed up to the aims of the project. In 1938 Madge made efforts to extend the network of volunteers beyond concentrations in industrial, mainland British towns and cities, and a Belfast cell was established.*

*The document transcribed below is amongst the papers of one of those who took part in the work of Mass Observation in Belfast in 1938. The questionnaire (Directive 4.38) issued was to be filled in on a particular day in April. The female correspondent was also the collator of the Belfast responses to Directive 4.38. In this document and, it would seem, for her own purposes, she has physically intercut her responses to questions in 'The Directive' with those of another correspondent in Belfast. She labels herself 'B' and the male correspondent 'A'.*

**Directive 4.38.**
As answered by A (shipping clerk, south of the city) and B (housewife, north of the city).

**(1) State your name, age, sex, marital status, politics, religion, *briefly*.**

A: 'A', aged 23. Male. Single. Atheist. Incline to left, when circumstances allow.

B: 'B', aged 26. Female. Married; one child.
*Politics:* Unionist, I suppose. I wish for more beneficence in public life.

*Religion:* Church-going, but not God-fearing.

**(2) What was your job/occupation on this day? If it was out of the ordinary, please state how.**

A: Clerk in shipping company. A normal day, ledgering cargoes in. Please advise for future Directives if last entries in (6) would be better here.

B: Housewife. I cooked, cleaned, shopped, educated my child, dealt with tradesmen, replied to letters, as a secretary would. A normal day.

**(3) Are you healthy? Did you have any particular health problems on the day in question?**

A: I am healthy. I do Müller's exercises on waking and before retiring, though on this day I omitted my night routine. I use the 1904 edition of *My System*. On the day in question I was well. Smoked too much, perhaps. In the evening, on returning home, I felt nauseous and a little disorientated. Hence no Müller's.

B: Quite healthy. Slight headache in the morning. Was woken early by son reciting nursery rhymes. Indigestion pm. A late evening for me, but felt well, if unable to sleep.

**(4) Describe the weather. Detail any dreams or nightmares.**

A: I confess that I never understand this category. Does Mr Madge believe that the weather on the Directive day affects my dreams from the previous night? The weather was overcast in the morning and there was light drizzle in the afternoon. A curious form of precipitation; small, persistent, almost sticky drops. I had dreams the previous night but, unfortunately, could not recall them on waking.

B: Weather grey, with some light rain. I dreamt that I was assistant to a man who was to give a lecture. I think I was married to him. The preamble of the dream was vague but I recall carrying his papers to the lectern as he watched me. He was adjusting his glasses, taking them off and polishing the lenses with a red handkerchief. As I tried to put the sheaf on the lectern it constantly slid and fell to the floor. I would then rearrange the pages and attempt to replace them in the correct order. As I shuffled them, though I did not read the words, I got the strong impression that his address was to be on the subject of modern sexuality and that he was, (1) going to embarrass himself by theorising on a topic of which he was ignorant, and (2) that it would be clear from his discourse that he was drawing on intimate details of our marriage. A blur then occurred in the dream. When the lecture began the man had transformed into a rather fierce figure, orating on the subject of political economy. I was relieved and tired, if it is possible to feel tired in a dream.

**(5) It is important to give a sense of the locale in which you spent your day. Outline any events or circumstances which might have coloured the local day and provide appropriate documentation.**

A: It being springtime, there was bunting on some of the streets as I walked to the office.

The newsstands had headlines which seemed, as always, to have a tone of excitement and fake dread about the probable war ahead. I have been reading some essays by Mr O---- recently (having seen in a leftist magazine that the Mr Madge has recommended Mr O---- as *the* writer for our times) and I have become properly sensitised to the loudhailer voice of the press.

There were an unusual number of ships entering the port today, and the tide favoured morning docking. It was a busy morning and I noticed little outside my work. Before lunch I had time to tally some of the figures for the last week's shipping. In the past few months I have occasionally looked through the ledger books to see if some pattern presaging war can be discerned from the movements of merchant vessels. I feel strongly that the authorities know more than the public about what the future holds.

The remainder of the day was devoid of any political nuance.

B: The morning radio talks constantly of foreign places now. I sometimes wonder whether they even exist. I repeat some of their names to my son over breakfast. I particularly like to hear him say the names of the Spanish towns.

In the evening my husband will always bring back the local paper and I read it when my son is in bed. On the letters page today there was another contribution in a long-running correspondence about the treatment of ex-servicemen from the last war. It seems that those who survived being gassed continue to suffer. I attach the cutting here.

The butcher's wife passed away three days ago, and my husband conducted her funeral service in the morning. There was a large gathering of neighbours and parishioners, though not so many as usual for a parish funeral. I am unsure why this was so.

**(6) Describe the events of your day (with times). Please be factual and concise. Record conversations verbatim. We wish to gather ordinary details, which may seem inconsequential to you.**

**Waking to Luncheon**

A: 7am. My mother woke me by knocking on my bedroom door. As with every morning, I lay still on my back for five minutes to consider the day ahead. Then I rose and went through my morning exercises. Breakfasted with my mother. No conversation of any worth. The radio babbled in the kitchen. I have tried to persuade my mother to listen to music, real music, rather than the jabbering of voices in the morning, but she will not change her habits. I left at 7.55am to walk to my workplace and arrived there at 8.35am, marginally late.

I had an extensive amount of paperwork to complete and that kept me busy until just before lunch. My supervisor made some sarcastic comments about me (11.30am) that he thought I could not hear. I did not respond.

B: 6.30am. My son rouses me each morning by jumping on my bed in time to 'Baa-baa Black Sheep'. His father's bed is never affected by this jolly wake-up call. My son and I cooked breakfast and we all three ate together. My husband went off to the parish office to prepare for the funeral. I cleaned the kitchen after breakfast and did some lessons with my child. He is almost reading independently now. He was so attentive at his lessons that I decided he should be rewarded with lunch out. On our way we passed by the funeral cortege. We took the tram to town at 11am and, having visited several stores, went for lunch in a café.

# Luncheon to the end of the working day

A: 1pm. I had to escort the Captain of a Moroccan vessel from its dock to the Office of Excises. The Office was, of course, shut for lunch at this hour but I had prior permission from my superior to dine with the Captain in a local café. The Captain spoke only French. I have studied French at night classes for the past two years. This was the first time I was able to use my new language skills! The Captain ate heartily at the company's expense. I talked to him about subjects which I thought would be of interest to him. To my disappointment, he had little opinion on the French colonial situation. I found his speech a little difficult to follow. His eating habits were not of the top order. At the end of the meal he became almost conspiratorial with me, and said several times a phrase I took to contain the word 'gueuse' as he gestured to our right. I had some memory of this word as meaning 'a mendicant' and I looked out the window to see to whom he was referring. I came to the realisation that he was staring rather unpleasantly at a young woman who was seated inside the café with her child. Together they were reading a book. I could tell, even through his Moroccan French, that some lewd inflection was being given to the phrase, and, having paid the bill and retained the receipt, I hurried him out of the café. As I passed by the café window I glanced back at the young lady. She was looking at me, timidly it seemed. For a moment I thought that she had tears in her eyes. By then, though, the rain had started and the windows were speckled with drizzle. She may not have been looking at me at all, but instead thinking of something else. I left, however, with the strong impression that her eyes were pleading with me.

2.15pm. I took the Captain to the Excise Office and waited for him outside the building. I smoked and thought. It was raining and unpleasant. The area outside the Excise Office is always windy because it turns its face to the harbour. By now my outer clothes were damp. The lady's eyes stayed in my thoughts, and this vision came back to me several times during the afternoon.

3.00pm. I returned to the office. My superior questioned how long it had taken me to deal with the Moroccan. I was angered by this suggestion of dalliance on my part. There was little to do in the afternoon, all the ships having docked early and there being nothing much due in until the next afternoon. Office conversation turned to horse racing and the pools. One of our number was delegated to go out to place bets when on 'toilet break'. I do not bet. As I have done before, I tried to point out to my colleagues the futility of gambling and the part that bookmaking plays in maintaining the class system. But whenever I attempt to turn the conversation with my fellow workers to anything serious I fail dismally. Ribaldry, it seems, is the best they are capable of.

B: My son and I had lunch in the café. I had bought him a new book, illustrated with trains and varieties of motor cars, and we looked at the pictures when we had finished eating. The café was rather dingy, and less welcoming than I remembered. I resolved not to go there again. We took the tram home, stopping at the greengrocer's. The butcher's shop, I had forgotten, was closed for the day and as I walked home, with my heavy bags, and my son weary from his trip to town, I felt a little sorry for myself, and wished once more that my husband's salary allowed for the luxury of a car. I was also anxious about what to cook for my husband's dinner.

## Evening

A: 5.30pm. I arrived home. My mother had tea prepared for my father and I. He returned at 5.45. I ate quickly since I was to go out for the evening.

6.30pm. I have recently been attending musical concerts by the Concert Orchestra. My friends have no interest in music, nor do my colleagues, so I attend these events alone. The audience which the Concert Orchestra attracts is the dregs of what this city can muster as a *petit bourgeoisie*. Nevertheless, the music is an oasis of cultural splendour in a town filled with Philistines. Last year they played a relatively new piece by Mr Britten. I left in good time and was there by 7.15pm. As I stood outside the hall, smoking, I noticed two women arriving and realised that one was the lady from the café at lunchtime. I went into the foyer thinking I could catch up with her and her companion and that I could apologise for the scene in the café. But I could not see her, nor her friend, and the bell was ringing for the beginning of the performance. I resolved to find her at the interval. The music was too Germanic for my taste. The second half was to be Sibelius.

8.15pm. At the interval I collected my cup of tea and looked through the crowd. I saw her sitting alone on a chair near the stairs. She seemed to have the same, somewhat melancholy look in her eyes as she had when I left the café. I hoped that she had not been dwelling on the Captain's vileness. The thought struck me that she too may have been a French speaker, and had understood him as well as I had. This only heightened my desire to ensure that she did not think badly of me. I will confess, if it is allowed, that I was also a little attracted by her. I introduced myself. 'I very much regret the behaviour which you were witness to at lunch today,' I said. Expressed in this way, I thought to distance myself from the Captain and show my concern for her. She seemed a little confused and asked me to explain. When I did she professed not to have noticed the Captain, nor indeed to recall having seen me in the café. It may have been that, by this ruse, she was saving me the embarrassment of further discussion of this painful subject. However, this left me unsure as to how to continue the conversation. Thankfully, she asked me how I had enjoyed the first half of the concert. 'Well enough,' I said, 'though I prefer slightly more modern music, and something a little less German.' She asked if I had a preference for the Russians. 'The English, actually,' I told her. 'He is, of course, sentimental, but I have a great liking for Vaughan Williams.' She asked if I had attended the performance of *Gerontius* some years before. 'It is a performance still talked about here, even these years later,' she said. 'But you are, perhaps, too young to have been here then.' I told her I had very much regretted missing the performance, despite my tender age at the time. The bell rang for the end of the interval, and her friend returned to her side. In a moment of impulsiveness, spurred perhaps by the sheer chance of meeting her twice on the same day, I asked her if she and her friend would have tea with me after the performance. As I asked the question, I felt in my pocket the coins I had with me and calculated that, if they ordered only tea, I could afford to live up to my invitation. They exchanged glances. The bell rang again. 'Yes,' she said. 'Very kind of you. Yes, of course.' We arranged to meet at the front door of the Hall, five minutes after the conclusion of the concert. The Sibelius pieces played by the Orchestra were stirring. 'Finlandia', in particular, I liked at the beginning, since it reminded me of Elgar. Later in 'Finlandia' the tune was the same as that of a hymn we sang at school, and I liked this much less.

9.20pm. The performance ended. I find the polite applause of the audience, and the feigned delight of the stiff-backed performers, unbearably middle-class. They like to imagine themselves in Mozart's Vienna, I think. On this occasion the guest conductor, a Swede, seemed to wish to ensure an especially long ovation for himself. The ritual of the classical concert should be a special object of study. I would be glad to take part in a specific Directive on this subject, and might have some ideas for its composition.

I left as quickly as I could and went to the front door. The lady and her friend were already there, in close conversation. I suggested that we go to a café nearby. They walked beside me, their arms linked. The young lady walked as if she were battling against a strong gust of wind, though it was a still evening. There was little conversation on the way there. We arrived at the café and sat down, the two ladies facing me. They discussed the concert. I found that I had, by this time, little to say about the music. Often the melodies are all that remain with me once I leave the Hall, and even these soon slip away into silence. The tea arrived. The lady's friend said, 'Enid, I really must be going,' though she looked at me as she said it. Enid (this is not her real name) replied that she would have to wait for half an hour or so, for the next tram. Her friend was take one of the new trolleybuses and had to leave immediately. 'Please, you go on,' said Enid. 'I'm sure,' she added, indicating me, 'that our new friend here will take care of me.' We two were left alone.

She asked me about my employment. I told her where I worked. I recounted how smothered I felt by the lack of intellectual companionship amongst my colleagues. I broadened the theme to include the whole town that we live in, its grimy walls and fettered consciousnesses. 'There must be other ways to live,' I said. She looked a little taken aback by the passion of my speech, but was also, I am certain, sympathetic. She asked me what I meant by 'other ways'. I told her that I read widely on politics, on religion, and on the science of psychoanalysis. I told her that last year, on my week's holiday, I had travelled to London to hear the great Mr A.H. deliver a series of evening lectures on 'The Present and Future State of *Homo Sapiens*', and of how he had opened my mind to the misery of provincial life and 'the alternative ways to be human' which would inevitably come in future decades. There would, A.H. had said, be new understandings of humans as economic actors and as sexual beings. As I said this last phrase I realised, with some pleasure, that I had never uttered the word 'sexual' before. I found myself saying it very confidently.

'How extraordinary,' she said. 'Yes, it is,' I went on, and extrapolated A.H.'s theory of sexual containment and the damage it does to the psyche. She asked me about A.H.; whether, that is, he was a competent lecturer, which seemed a little by-the-by. She also asked me what he looked like, which is even less germane to his ideas. But, as she asked these things, her eyes were gleaming in the café lights. That look of sad oppression which I had seen earlier in the day had been replaced by something else. It was a wonderful moment. She was listening to what I was saying.

She glanced at her watch. 'I must leave to get my tram. It really has been very kind of you to look after me in this way. I am most intrigued by our meeting.' She shook my hand and I held on to hers for as long as decency would allow. 'Will we meet again?' I asked her. 'I am certain we shall,' she said. 'I absolutely must be leaving.' She buttoned her coat and then undid the clasp on her handbag to find her purse. I noticed, in her bag, the distinctive blue paper of a Directive. 'You are an Observer too,' I said. 'Ever more extraordinary,' she said. 'Fate, it seems, has brought us together tonight. Goodbye.' She left in a hurry, to get her tram from beside the City Hall.

11.30pm. I am writing this Directive at the end of the day while its events are fresh in my mind. I walked home from the café. I was in a state of some excitement. Enid seemed to me to be a breath of hope in an otherwise hostile world. I know that she is married and has a child. However, I am also convinced that some things in this life meet us with a force that cannot be restrained by convention alone.

B: 5.45pm. My husband returned home. He and my son discussed the events of the day while I finished cooking their dinner. From the kitchen I could hear my son asking why the butcher's wife had died. My husband reassured him that God had wanted the butcher's wife to come to heaven.

My husband had forgotten that I was going to a concert in the evening. He was rather short-tempered at the thought of having to put our son to bed by himself. For a time I thought that I might have to cancel the evening out. However, peace prevailed. I left the two of them pondering the new picture book we had bought earlier in the day and took the tram back to town. I found the conversation between the two women who sat in the seats on front of me entertainingly colloquial, though I'm afraid I have rather forgotten the exact language of it now. They complained of their husbands, that I remember, and how they were 'never out of' the pub.

I met my friend at the doors of the Concert Hall. We were just in time and rushed to our usual seats (we have season tickets). The music was glorious. At the interval my friend went off to the ladies' room and I sat down in the foyer. Despite the hubbub of talk it was lovely to have a moment to myself. I found myself remembering my school days because I caught the glance of a lady whose face reminded me of a girl who shared my dorm. A young man introduced himself to me. I did not recognise him, but he told me that he had seen me earlier in the day in the café with my son. He suggested that the man he was with, who was, it turned out, a foreigner, had possibly said something unpleasant *about me* in the café. I was very perplexed by this, and a little discomfited by the young man. He spoke as though he had just finished a bad elocution lesson and he stared very intently at me between sentences. Sometimes the pauses were really quite long. When my friend rejoined me I could see that she noticed his oddness too. Quite of out the blue he asked us to join him for tea after the concert. I could think of nothing else to say other than to accept.

9.15pm. The concert finished. We waited outside for the young man. I could tell that my friend thought it improper for the two of us, both married ladies, to be having tea with a young man. It took a few minutes for him to join us. I expect the crowds on the stairs meant that it was some time before he could get downstairs. We walked the short distance to the café he had suggested. We were over-dressed in comparison to the rest of the clientele, and my friend became more formal than she usually is as a result. This is, perhaps, a typical reaction to being in close proximity to those of a lower social standing? Finally I think it was too much for her and she found the excuse that the new trolleybus times meant that she had to leave. I knew this not to be the case, but I did not challenge her. I had begun to find her truculence with the young man to be rude. No matter about his abrupt manner, he did not deserve unkindness.

When she left the young man sat in silence. He stirred his tea vigorously and I felt a little sorry for him. I asked him if he worked. So many men these days have no employment. As if released from some social bind, he began to talk rapidly, complaining about the 'idiocy' of those who shared his office.

He had taken off his overcoat and I noticed that the elbows of his jacket were worn to a shine. From deskwork, no doubt. He also had ink stains on the first two fingers of his left hand. His monologue continued without a break. He talked of his mother and of his attempts to educate himself. He had taken a trip to London to attend a series of lectures by a writer of whom I had never heard. This seemed to me rather unusual behaviour for an office boy. He was talking really quite loudly by this time, and I found it somewhat embarrassing to be sitting with him. He summarised the lectures given by the writer. As he did so my dream from the previous night came back to me and seemed to overlap almost exactly with his description of the content of the lecture series. I told him I thought that this was an extraordinary coincidence. As he talked I tried to recall to my mind's eye the face of the man who, in my dream, I was married to.

I realised that it was time to leave for my tram. As I took my purse from my bag the young man noticed this Directive. (My husband would not, I think, entirely approve of my participation in the Observations, so I keep Directive forms to myself). The young man told me that he too was an Observer. I imagined the amusement of those who read these reports when they realised that two Observers had met.

11.30pm. I arrived home. My husband was already asleep. I sat in the kitchen with a mug of cocoa. I began compiling this report. The music from the concert is still in my ears, along with the voice of the young man. When we parted he had asked if we would meet again. I should that we would, of course. We are both, after all, concertgoers. I wonder now if he might have misconstrued my words? But I hardly think so. On my way home I mulled over the strange coincidence of my dream and his description of the lectures in London. I long to enter that dreamworld once more, but I know that when I go to bed I will lie flat on my back for hours, waiting for sleep to come.

*Colette Bryce*

## Don't speak to the Brits, just pretend they don't exist

Two rubber bullets stand on the shelf,
from Bloody Sunday – mounted in silver,

space rockets docked and ready to go off;
like the Sky Ray Lolly that crimsons your lips

when the orange Quencher your brother gets
attracts a wasp that stings him on the tongue.

'Tongue' is what they call the Irish language,
'native tongue' you're learning at school.

Kathleen is sent home from the Gaeltacht
for speaking English, and it's there

at the Gaeltacht, ambling back
along country roads in pure darkness

that a boy from Dublin
talks his tongue right into your mouth,

holds you closely in the dark and calls it
French kissing (he says this in English).

# The Republicans

Their walls are like any other walls, muffled in layers of paste and paper.
Squares compete with a carpet's swirls. The room is a-clutter with adolescents,
children, ashtrays, dirty cups; a television's flash and jabber.

A man reclines in an armchair, dragged up close to the hearth, his feet
on the shelf. Glowing coals are banked with slack. Cooking smells waft in
from beyond the door. Two schoolgirls braid each other's hair.

Jesus opens his ruptured chest in a frame; in another, Jesus again
at an earlier age, in his mother's arms. In a third, a triptych in household gloss
depicts a map, a gun, and a dove. *Ireland unfree shall never be at peace*,

spelled out by sons in prison workshops. The republicans
rest their plates on their knees and gobble up their dinners, quickly.
Mince. Potatoes. Peas or beans. They light their fags and inhale, deeply.

# North to the South

1

The map unfolded in the car
like a kite, a barely
controllable thing
to be wrestled, my father
overcome.

A giant's hands
might have practised origami,
a bird, or a boat
on which an impossible dream
might stay afloat.

2

A head through the window
on the driver's side.

Where have we come from?
Where are we going?

Eight little girls and a dog
spill out.

Aunty Máire was famous
for spelling out her name

P-Ó-G M-O T-H-Ó-I-N,
which they duly wrote down.

3

You are giving the vast Atlantic
to your father, bucketful
by bucketful, padding

to and fro on the damp strand
to store it at his feet
in a hole where

it only appears to vanish.

Daniel Shand

# Layover

The woman leans into the taxi and gives the driver a folded note. He unfolds it between two fingers. 'This is French,' he says with a thick accent.

'Goodness. So it is,' says the woman and produces a new one from her handbag. The notes are passed between them and he holds the new bill up to the light from the streetlamp that buzzes above the taxi. He nods and reaches down and she can hear the clunk of the boot's lock being released.

A moment later she stands on the pavement and looks at the building before her, a suitcase on either side. She brings a brass cigarette holder out from the pocket of her mackintosh and slides free an impossibly narrow cigarette. She lights it and looks up at the name of the hotel, lit up in red and blue fluorescent. 'Oh Muriel,' she exhales and as her eyes follow the rising smoke she notices a movement in the curtains behind a balcony two floors up. She hears a glass bottle rolling on hard floor.

'Call again,' she says, louder this time. 'Keep calling until she picks up.'

The young man behind reception runs his hand through his curly hair. He glances towards the cluster of guests by the bar in the next room. 'I've called five times.'

She tuts and scowls and reaches across the counter, bangs the phone down in front of her. 'The phone is only for members of staff,' says the young man.

'Please don't be ridiculous,' she says. 'A phone is a phone. How does this work? What is the extension?'

He swallows. He hears laughter from the bar. 'I'm not supposed to say.'

'My daughter is a guest in your hotel. I have reason to believe she may be in serious danger. If you won't tell me the number then I'll have no choice but to hold you personally responsible should any danger befall her, Alexander.'

He tells her the number and a thick thumbprint of red blossoms across the bridge of his nose. She dials in the number, 1509, lets it ring three times, hangs up and then dials again. She hears a click and the soft wet breath of her daughter in her ear. 'Muriel?' says the woman.

No answer.

'Muriel?' A pause. 'Right,' she says and replaces the receiver. She stares at the phone for a beat, two, and then lets out the shallowest of sighs. 'Thank you Alexander,' she says, looking up. 'You have been a great help.'

He nods, the blush intensifying, noticing the darkness of her eye shadow.

All along the walls of the corridor are paintings of ships – ferries and paddle steamers, ocean liners and yachts. The woman walks by them without seeing, her head and neck rigid. Up ahead she sees a man reverse out of one of the rooms. He is pulling on a jacket. The door slams in his face. He slaps at the door and then shrugs before turning and walking towards the woman, muttering something in a language she doesn't understand, reeking of alcohol and cheap, cheap deodorant.

The woman knows the number of the room he left before she reaches it. 1509.

Muriel feels the knock before it comes, the way that skin prickles before it is even touched. A tart, vicious knock. She turns in the chair and looks at the door before scraping the last of the stuff from the mirror and into a pencil tin. She closes the tin and places it in the bottom drawer of the dresser alongside a wrapped bundle of bank notes and a large silver locket.

The knock comes again. The curtains quiver and show a sliver of night from the balcony. 'Coming,' says Muriel. She looks at herself in the mirror of the dresser and rubs a thick smear of blusher into each hollow cheek. She purses and turns her head from side to side and gets up out of the chair. She walks across the room and places her hand and the side of her face against the door and listens. Nothing. She chews her thumbnail and looks around the room, the bed unmade, the bottle she dropped on its side. A cold room.

On the other side of the door the woman is in the same position, ear resting on the door, hearing only the breath in her nose and her heart beat in the canals of her head. She taps her long nails against the wood, listens to what sounds like a thump by the time each tap reaches her ear.

The door opens slowly and she stands back, upright. Muriel is there, wearing a pearlescent nightdress. 'Well,' says the woman, through a breath.

'Hello,' says Muriel.

'It's good to see you dear.'

'I didn't know you were in town. You should have called.'

'I did call,' says the woman. 'I called up, from reception.'

'There must have been an issue in the lines,' says Muriel and the woman raises her eyebrows.

'Well, I suppose there must have been. Aren't you going to ask me in?'

Muriel nods and opens the door wider. The woman enters and Muriel closes it behind her. 'What a gorgeous space,' says the woman looking around. 'This must cost. Well anyway, you get what you pay for don't you?'

'Would you like a drink?'

The woman sits down on the edge of bed, brushing aside a pair of tights. 'Yes. A vodka tonic.'

'With ice?'

'With ice.'

The girl goes into the next room to make the drinks. 'How is Paris?' she says loudly.

'Very nice,' says the woman. 'Very cold. Jerome's show is doing very well you know. Very well indeed.'

Muriel stands in the doorway holding a glass in each hand. 'Oh,' she says. 'Good.' She places her own drink down on the dresser and hands the other to her mother who takes it from her and holds her by the hand before Muriel can pull away.

'Your hand is cold,' says the woman.

'The ice.'

'Of course,' she says, letting it go. 'Do you mind if I smoke?'

'No. Of course.'

The woman lights another narrow cigarette and leans back on one arm. The girl sits down at the dresser and turns so her mother can see her, in profile. 'My little girl. How are you, Muriel? How are you? I notice the suite has a piano. Are you working?'

'A little, when the mood takes me.'

'I'm so lucky, to be surrounded by such talented people.'

'Yes.'

Ice rattles in each glass as they both drink and glance around the room. Neither of them speaks for a full minute.

'How long are you here for?' says Muriel, looking her mother in the eye for the first time.

'A few hours at most. I'm flying out again tonight.'

'I see,' says Muriel and she finishes her drink and stands up.

'I wish I could stay longer dear, I really do.'

'Another?'

'Yes,' says the woman, holding up her glass. Muriel takes it from her and disappears again into the next room.

'I wish you could come out and stay with us a while,' says the woman. 'It would be good for you, don't you think?'

'Yes, I suppose it would be,' says Muriel's voice. 'But I'm just so busy here. And besides, you know I can't stand Jerome.'

The woman closes her eyes and kicks off her shoes. 'I wish you would give him a chance, it has been fifteen years since your father passed.'

'I know how long it's been,' says Muriel in the doorway.

'When are you going to get your own place?'

'I don't know.'

'I see.'

They finish their second and third drinks in near silence. Muriel takes a cigarette from her mother's holder and they both smoke. They catch each other's eye. The woman smiles and Muriel looks away. The woman notices how thin her daughter looks. How drawn. 'Are you taking your medication dear?'

Muriel nods.

'Good. Good.'

What a girl. What a girl. The angriest baby in the whole maternity unit. The angriest girl in the whole school. Never to be seen without a scowl. 'May I?' she says gesturing to the balcony.

Muriel nods.

The woman leans on the balcony, facing into the room. The doorway frames Muriel sitting at the dresser. She turns her head up to see dark clouds racing between her and stars. 'What a night.'

'You'll catch cold,' says Muriel.

'That's alright,' says the woman.

'Is there something wrong?'

'I don't believe there is,' she says, producing the cigarette holder.

Muriel looks at the swirls and eyes in the rich wood of the dresser's top. 'Why did you come here? I thought that I made myself clear in my letter.'

The woman laughs. 'You want me to just cut you off Muriel? Jesus.'

'Please don't laugh at me. You don't get to laugh at me.'

The woman waves her cigarette. 'Sure. Sure,' she says. 'I'm sorry.' She pulls the collar of her raincoat together at the neck with her free hand. 'I don't feel like it's good for us not to speak my dear. I don't think it's healthy for either of us, but especially not for you.'

Muriel taps at the dresser with her cigarette lighter. She pulls back the lid and snaps it shut, releasing gusts of sweet smelling vapour. 'Ok.'

The woman comes back inside. 'What a beautiful city,' she says as she resumes her seat at the base of the bed. 'When can we start being a family again?'

'We haven't been a family for five years,' says Muriel, closing the lighter with a hard slap. 'I wasn't the family you were interested in continuing.'

'That's not fair.'

'Tell me about it.'

'I'll make us a drink.'

The woman makes the drinks in the next room, plucking perfect cubes of ice from the bucket with tongs, dropping in thick wedges of lemon that sizzle as they plunge into the glass. Muriel watches her from her perch at the dresser.

People said she had her mother's mouth. A luscious, sarcastic pair of lips. How irritating. A person you loved despite anything. What hard work it was, to be angry. Exhausting and unfulfilling. And besides, Muriel was getting very, very tired.

The woman re-enters and hands the drink to Muriel. 'We did OK didn't we kid? Ten years on our own?'

Muriel lowers her eyes. The woman smiles. 'I thought so.'

A much warmer silence incubates the drinking and finishing of their fourth round. They finish at the same time and place their glasses onto the plush salmon carpet.

'Can I. Can I see?' says the woman, gesturing to Muriel's head.

Muriel raises her hand to the back of her skull and pats the hair there.

'Please?'

Muriel nods and climbs down from the dresser to shimmy across the floor to the space between her mother's legs. Turning away and resting her arms on her knees she begins to feel fingers parting her hair at the crown of her scalp. Checking for headlice. Bonding gorillas.

The woman finds the scar quickly, a long pink smile running along the curve of Muriel's scalp. She lifts the hair up from it and traces it with the finger of the other. 'Poor baby.' Both woman look up and see themselves in the mirror.

'Tell me about it again.'

'Oh Muriel. I don't like to think about it my dear.'

'Please.'

The woman smoothes the hair back down over the scar. 'You don't remember a thing?'

'Nothing.'

'Well,' she says, smoothing the hair, lifting it and letting it fall and twisting it into little tight bunches. 'You recall the car at least?'

'A little.'

'It was a beautiful car you know. I can see that now.'

'How did it look?'

'It was a convertible and the colour was green. Dark green. I don't remember the make. It was his pride and joy, apart from you of course. Every Sunday he would rub beeswax into the bonnet and we would go out for a drive. I would put my hair up in a bandana. Until you came along of course.'

Muriel rests her neck on her mother's thigh. 'Why?'

'Because it was tiny my dear. Just two seats. You cannot go careering around the countryside with a tot on your lap. No we got something much more sensible, but he did keep hold of it. Until you were older, he said.'

'And then that day. That spring morning.'

'April fool's,' says Muriel, the weight of her skull increasing with each of her mother's claps.

'April fool's. He took you out for your first drive. You were so excited, do you remember? No, of course. I waved you off and then, then I got the call two hours later.' She listens to the heaviness of her daughter's breaths, feels her open mouth press into her stockings. 'It was a mystery how you survived. And your poor father, dead at the wheel and your locket. Well. Anyway. What a waste. They found the two of you out by the mill, the car was on its roof in a ditch.

'I saw the photo – maps and driving gloves and deer you hit all over the road. I came to you in the hospital. You woke up and you had no idea where you were, what had happened. You were trying to sit up, giggling from the anaesthetic and your poor head all wrapped up.'

Muriel quivers slightly, an involuntary shudder that tells the woman her daughter is dreaming. She tucks the hair behind her ear, leans in and kisses her on the lobe. 'There there.'

The woman leaves her daughter sleeping lightly on top of the unmade bed, her hands palm up by her ears as if in surrender. She considers the room soberly, taking in the gauche Greco-Roman decorations, and the smaller details too. Surreptitious bottles lurking behind flower vases and candlesticks, tiny plastic bags screwed up and stuffed between mattress and frame, beneath pages of blank sheet music with the bars alternately coloured in with black felt tip. Again, the shallowest of sighs.

She stands and walks towards the bathroom, running a nail along the wall as she does. The chill from the cold white tile – her green eyes scan the room; torn shower curtain, lipstick on mirror, wine and medicine bottles by sink. A good white: Italian. She crosses the floor, arching her feet to avoid the cold. More bottles, piled in the sink. Each of them empty.

She looks at herself in the mirror. 'Oh Muriel.'

*Rody Gorman*

## Timberwoodmaterialcontrivancevigouryewlogy: Dear Little Horny Pricket Lowbraybellowfellow

Dear little horny pricket lowbraybellowfellow, dear little horny gluttonbawler of the sweetcliffgableregardhornpeaks, your tuftembracebundlefalsettocuckooquaichtalksinging in the smokecloudglenhollow is cliffgableMcpeakeregardsweet to us. Hiraeth for my own wee place came upon my wits, the herbplants on the battleplainfield, the Ossianicfawns in the Jovemoormountain. Dronebushy leafy treeoghamDbulloak, you're hillockhighloud above penisvault-trees, little treeoghamCwordcastrationhazel, little heatherembellishmentbranchtree,cofferof treeoghamCwordhazelnuts. Far-from-enemy-like treeoghamFwordpolealder, your licksheen is delightfulbeautiful, no indifference-shapeappearance of knify hawthornbushes in the gap where you are. Dearlittle bristleblackthorn, dearlittle broochpinthorn, dearlittle black glandsloe, bloodtracebrooklimewatercress, hindrancecreamcroptop of lockgreygreen bellfinch-coalfish-sealettuce from the hosteldentbrink, of the elklullblackbird's wellfountain. Parsley piert of the Connor Pass deermountainpassway, you're the flatterhoneysweetest herbplant, bellfinch-coalfish-sealettuce, speechtune-screereefbranchtuftflowerchoice of bellfinch-coalfish-sealettuce, plantherb raspberryjam-suckjuice grows on. Dearlittleyoung lampoonerprickerbramble, dearlittleyoung ridgebackflower, you don't do me right, you never stop lacerating me until you've had your tidefull of mettleblood. Newry yew, you dearlittle yew you, starappearing in relicgraveyards, ivy, dearlittle ivy, your usual habitat is the dark waxy castrationwood. Holly, dearlittle sheltered one, valveshutter-doorleaf in the airbreathwind, ash tidefull of evilspirit-harm, armyarm of a laymanherowarrior's armhands. Beingbeech, blossomsmooth and blessed, dearlittle cliffgableregardhornpeaksweet swellsurge, every tied heatherembellishmentbranchtree on the summit of your headend is delightbeautiful shake-aspen penisvault-tree trembleshaking shaketremblingly, I hear turns about its leaf's running, that's a cattle-raidplunderloss. I hate the fathombeechwoods, I make no bones about it, shootsproutsapling of leafy treeoghamDbulloaks always on the go. A bad omen how I contraryruined Ronan Finn McBerry's hospitalityhonour, his tomb-miracles giving me grief, his vesicleclusterclockbells from the cellchurchyard. A bad omen how I found Conall's bannerarms, his favourite tunic omencovered in gold. The nimblebold fairyarmycrowd all said don't let the man with the delightbeautiful tunic shunfleefly from you aroundunder the kyle-narrow Jovecoverthicket. Jinkscrapstingwound and deadkill, take advantage of him, put him, good enough for his guiltsins, on a waterspike and a gablepoint. The cornsprout-horsemen catching up on me across frugalround Moycove, not one shot from them will reach my beamridgeback. Going through the ivybranches, I don't hide, I'm like a noblegood shot from a javelinspear going with the airbreathwind. Dearlittle doe, dearlittle tracker, I've gotten bitehold of you, I'm cornsprout-riding you from every sweetcliffgableregardhornpeak where I am. From Carncornan to the sweetcliffgableregardhornpeak of Slievenanee, from the sweetcliffgableregardhornpeak of Slievillion I reach the Galtees in Iffa and Offa. From the Galtees to Carnliffeylurk, I come before afternoonevening to saltbitter Benbulben. At night before Conall's batallionbattle I was happy, before I bedragglefumblebumbled, seektraversing the sweetcliffgableregardhornpeaks. Glenbalkan is my steadypermanent wombabode where I got a gripbite, many a night I asktried to run up the sweetcliffgableregardhornpeak. If I seektravelled on my tod all the moormountains of the Jovenobletimberbrown world-domain, I would rather the place for one coopcabin in frugalround Glenbalkan. Its shrillweedclear lockgreygreen urineraintearswater is noblegood, its fierce shrillweedclear airbreathwind is noblegood, its watercress and lockgreygreen hindrancecreamtopcrop is noblegood, best of all is the hillockhigh brooklime there. It's hardy ivybushes are noblegood and its shrillweedclear treeoghamS-sallies, it's yewy yew from the Lordship of Newry is noblegood, best of all its cliffgableregardhornpeaksweet beingbeech. If you were to come, Lynchehaun, to me in any ghostform, every night to talk to me, maybe I wouldn't stopwait for you. I wouldn't stopwait for your conversation were it not for the storynews which lionsprainwounded me, father, mother, son, young girldaughter, brother, down-pourstrong womanwife all croaked. If you were to come to talk to me, I wouldn't be the better for it, I would seektravel the sweetcliffgableregardhornpeaks of the Mourne Moormountains before matunination. By the mealfragment mill, your rural-laitytribe was pendantblubber-ruined, tired saddo, earlyfast Lynchehaun. Hag of the mill, why would you want to get at me with deceit? I hear you giving me grief out on the mountain. Hag, roundhead, would you go on a steedhorse? I would, chunky chappy, if I didn't see any apparitionperson. If I did, Sweeney, here's to my jumping. If you don't, hag, may you lose your wits. What you're saying isn't right but, Coleman from Kilcash. Wouldn't I be the better horseperson, not falling back? What I say is right enough, hag without a titter of wit, destroyed by a demon, you've destroyed yourself. Wouldn't you be the better for my anticart, leanmean grazingnakedwoodlunatic, with me stickfollowing you from the summit of the sweetcliffgableregardhornpeaks? A tuft of lonelyproudspiritedrank ivy growing through a twisted penis-shaftvault-tree, if I was in the top I'd be afraid to come out. I antifadgeflee the skylarks talehousewandertravelling at tightfull stretch, I leap over the tall-stemmedgrassreedstalks from the summit of the cliffgableregardhornpeaks. The poxtroutspeckled ivybush turtledove, when it rises up for us, it doesn't take me long to overtake it since I grew egretfoliagehairfeathers. The Oscarignorant devilgadfly-haywoodcock when it rises up to me, the elklullblackbird when it makes its highpitchedcall is a truered enemy as far as I'm concerned. Every hourtime I leap till I'm on the groundearth I see the little sacrumfox down there erodegnawing reefstripbones. More than any championIrishwolfhound in the ivybush, he'd would overtake met, I would jump just as ashfast to the sweetcliffgableregardhornpeak. Foxcubs gluttonbawling this way and that, landsonwolves pertgossipsmiting, I shunflyflee the sound they make. They cametried to overtake me but I shunfled to the hillockhighloud summit of the sweetcliffgableregardhornpeaks. My elopementgaitgoing is brought to a territory-end whichever deermountainpassway I go, it's clear from my remorse that I'm a sheep without a pen. The sacredscionbordertree in Killowe where I sleep quietpeacefully, better than in Conall's moonspacetime the furyassemblyfair in tidefull Moylinny. Starry frost will come and rain on every generationpool, I'm lostwandering, lying helplessly on my back on the sweetcliffgableregardhornpeak. The oddroundcraneherons calling in rawcold Glenelly, an ashfast flock of teenyweenySweenybirds this way and that. I don't like the dizzybuzzing that men and wifewomen make, the vanishgreetcelebrationfarewellwarble that the elklullblackbird makes hillockhighloud is cliffgableregardhornpeaksweeter to me. I don't like the scroungetrumpeting that I hear earlyearly, the crocking of the messbadger in Beenabrack is cliffgableregardhornpeaksweeter to me. I don't like the hornblowing I hear tightnear, the rutbellowing that the oxenstag with two severalscore peakhorns makes is cliffgableregardhornpeaksweeter to me. There's the makings of a sixyokeploughteam in every smoke-cloudglenhollow, every oxenstag lying down on the top of the sweetcliffgableregardhornpeaks. Though there's a multitude of oxenstags in every smoke-cloudglenhollow, it's rarely the armhand of a satirewhipherd fortressencloses their peakhorns. The oxenstag of the hillockhighloud Slieve Felim Mountains, the oxenstag of the wild Fews, the oxenstag of Duhallow, the oxenstag of Orrery, the fierce oxenstag of Lough Leane. The oxenstag of Islandmagee, the Late Larnian oxenstag of Larne-in-Lorne, the oxenstag of Moylinny, the oxenstag of Cooley, the oxenstag of Cunghill, the oxenstag of the twinhornpeaked Burren. Mother of the horse-stud, your beermantle has turned grey, there isn't an oxenstag after you that doesn't have two severalscore peakhorns. More than the stuff for a shirt, my own endhead has turned grey, if I was on every sweetpeaklet there would be a peaklet on every one. Oxenstag making that noise at me across the smoke-cloudglenhollow, that's a noblegood shelfspace on the summit of your cliffgableregardpeakhorns. I'm Shivna the begforage-seektraveller, I go faster than Senna across the smoke-cloudhollowglens, that's not my proper designation, more like Horny Devil Mountainy Man. The best wellfountain of them all is the wellfountain of Laydlaun, the most delighbeautiful tow-barwellfountain is the spring of Dunmail. Though I've made many an emigrationflitting, my sailclothes today have been cut short, I'm always on watch in the summit of the sweetcliffgableregardhornpeaks. Bracken, roserussetred treeoghamFwordpostalder, your beermantles have turned grey, there's no litterbedding for a proscribed man in the creekcrotch of your sweetcliffgableregardpeaks. My worldlife will be rightadjacentsouth in Taiten and angelic St Mullin's, that's where I'll lose all hornpeakregard. What's made me obliged to you is Ronan Finn's curse, dearlittle horny pricket one, dearlittle lowbraybellowfellow, gablesweet gluttonbawler.

# Reviews

*Collected Poems*. Carcanet, 995pp, ISBN 978 1 847771 26 1. £25
Edward Dorn

In several key ways Ed Dorn's magisterial *Collected Poems* is a bridge between the late Modernist milieu of Black Mountain poetics within which he began writing (and which he almost immediately reacted against), and the conceptually various landscape of contemporary American – and by extension, English-speaking – poetry.

From the Poundian matrices of Charles Olson toward and beyond the politically radicalised syntax of the Language poets is a long way to have travelled, but this most emblematic of US poets was always a chronicler of intellectual journeys, an historian of discourses, whether within a poem or across cultures, through inner space or into political denunciation. As he says in his 1974 preface to a previous *Collected Poems*, 'From near the beginning I have known my work to be theoretical in nature and poetic by virtue of its inherent tone.'

In three key periods – the early 60s work, the epic masterpiece *Gunslinger*, and the posthumous collection *Chemo Sâbe* – Dorn developed new ways of considering American idioms (including those of political power and the media), cultural history both as myth and repressive force, and twentieth century Modernism's fascination with (and fetishisation of) the long poem. No small achievement, especially set beside the fact that his wit, an important source of his intellectual energy, makes him singularly approachable.

One surprise new readers of Dorn will perhaps experience at the outset is the role played by Britain and British writers in his earlier work. As J.H. Prynne puts it in a warm and insightful afterword:

> ...he spent a good deal of his middle-formative time in England, and that's rather exceptional for American writers...many [of whom] couldn't at all tune in to, and understand, and accept even the distinctive voices of their English forebears and contemporaries.

Both the ability to listen and absorb other voices, and the reluctance to align himself with orthodoxies, even radical orthodoxies, mean that in his earlier work Dorn is constructing and compositing, augmenting his own distinctive cadences and territories with those of others and other cultures. In 'Sousa', from his first collection, he already knows the music of nostalgia carries its own contradiction:

> Great brass bell of austerity
> and the ghosts of old picnickers
> ambling under the box elder when the sobriety
> was the drunkenness…

While in the 1965 collection *Geographies* (dedicated to Olson), a desacralised America is depicted in terms that restate Eliot for a newly permissive society:

> …american men
> who may no longer wear the bottoms of their trousers rolled
> but who are certainly all circumcised without ritual
> and wear the ends of their penises rolled…

His stay in England brings references to Harwood and Pickard – his influence on the latter and Barry MacSweeney via his trip to the Morden Tower being noteworthy in this context, and the landscape of the North-East allows him to create a significant historical footnote:

> Note: if the americans built a wall
>     in Vee-et (past tense of ate)
>     NAM, they would at least leave
>     something behind as *made* – the
>     way stations could even have Texan
>     inscription…

– an idea which seems to predict Geoffrey Hill's use of anachronism in *Mercian Hymns*. In the same collection and in the same country, the idea for *Gunslinger* (already implicit in the 1964 collection *Hands Up!*) crystallises after seeing *The Magnificent Seven*:

> Tom remarked, on the evidence of
> the last scene when the Mexican-
> Japanese said Vaya con Dios
> and Yul said a simple adios,
> 'that was philosophical'.

*Gunslinger*'s premiss is simple enough, that the mythologising of the Western, having absorbed other cultures into it and been exported back to those cultures, offers a ripe allegory for Western values. Its execution, however, is dazzling. A comic oratorio for a series of counter cultural voices and their opposites, it admits a number of tropes from cinema – including, in Book 1's recurrent form of capitalised 'strum's, soundtrack – as well as parodies of song, hints of Elizabethan and later English lyrical poetry, endless stoned and psychedelic puns, a fissiparous 'I' which it rapidly becomes clear both can and cannot be identified with the poet, and, of course, a talking horse:

> *My god, Slinger,* she said
> I am at your service,
> replied the Gunslinger.
> *Oh knock that off!*
> *I've got a Business to tend to*
> *and the smoke in this corner*
> *is blindin besides, say*
> *haven't I met that Horse*
> *before?* The Horse
> rose from his chair and
> tipped his stetson XX
> Hello £ill, it's been a long time
> here have a seat,
> we've got a lot to talk
> about, *Slow down*
> the Gunslinger said and
> that was the only time
> I ever heard anybody speak
> obliquely to the Horse.

The poem is full of typographical play, so it's an especial delight of this edition that it reproduces as an appendix the *Bean News*, a kind of newspaper, which shadows the text like an allusion to journalism's way with history in *The Man Who Shot Liberty Valance*.

*Gunslinger* changes the frame of reference of the American long poem as we understand it from *The Cantos*, Olson's *Maximus Poems*, or Carlos Williams's

*Paterson*, in that there is a redefinition of Poundian *paideuma*: this is not an epic which seeks to re-educate us about history, or reconnect us to culture. That doesn't mean it eschews the dimension of moral critique of contemporary society which access to the historical imagination validates.

Its real achievement is rather to remove the hierarchical distinction between historical example and how history is portrayed, discussed and distorted in the parallel cultural fields of cinema, the press, genre fiction, and cartoons, etc. Its primary means of doing this, the 'virtue of its inherent tone' is still, arguably, pure Pound: what he called *logopoeia*, or 'the dance of the intellect among words', which 'takes count in a special way of habits of usage, of the context we expect to find with the word.' Or, as Taco Desoxin puts it:

> We also supply Hi-grade lunatic information
> *you can get it here* & so forth
> also do Pre-pourd Scorn, that's on
> twenty-four hours notice

*Gunslinger*, then, works by manipulating registers and creating tensions between different discourses. This simultaneously brings us into the media-saturated latter half of the twentieth century, and risks stranding us there. An element of the delight of Gunslinger now rests in its depiction of a period. The self-obfuscating exchanges of its stoned heroes may become as quaint as they are (occasionally) protracted, and time will have to tell us if it can transcend this.

However, the dissolving and reforming narrative voices seem to prefigure the refusal of a singular coherent referentiality we find in Language poetry. Furthermore, its influence extends beyond the US, and can be seen, for instance, in the poetry of Andrew Grieg, whose early work, particularly *Men On Ice*, uses dialogue between allegorical figures in a similar manner to play out his metaphysical exploration of mountain climbing.

The latter part of Dorn's writing returns his focus firmly to the historical in unfinished sequences like *Languedoc Variorum*, and, in *Captain Jack's Chaps*, his account of an outing to a literary gathering in Houston, the horseplay of *Gunslinger* appears to be played out again, but with named individuals ('We debouch into the lobby. There's Marj Perloff/confident and bright, but not overdone.')

The difficulty with this is a marked drop in satiric subtlety, as in 'Self

Criticism', in which a Republican mindset sets forth a repellant credo, but the poet seems have lost interest in both character and voice: 'I will approve of genocide in Central America/because it is proprietary…'.

Tragically, it takes the diagnosis of terminal pancreatic cancer to restore Dorn's vision in several senses of that term. Firstly, he writes descriptively again with a shrewd eye for the ideologies underlying ordinary phenomena:

> Big red balloon tethered over Cub Food
> winterpale shoppers, struggling with the load
>
> like overweight ants dragging their take
> away from an abandoned sandwich
>
> A long ghost-white buick idles at the zebra
> black glass, chrome gone, white tires
>
> A deal in every aisle, every hour, every day…

Secondly, having to take an intimidating range of powerful drugs, he notates their mind-altering qualities in striking terms:

> Decadron sharpens the senses
> around the optic nerve and the neo cortex,
> enabling one to see through walls and into
> the present – there goes the Pope, mobile as ever –
> …as the drip is connected to the pump I see W.J. Clinton
> full humping St. Monicka panting in the pantry…

Finally, in a gesture which will remind a Scottish reader of Edwin Morgan's marvelous dialogue between a cancer cell and its healthy equivalent, 'Gorgo and Beau', he gives allegorical life to his own tumour: 'She's like Wittgenstein's lunch, utterly invariable,/ *and* she's like your own private third world…' – that last line, implying we're all moral conservatives when it comes to the body, shows that Dorn's wit as well as his imagination has triumphed over his disease.

The tumour can therefore be seen as a terrible but normal part of the body's geography, and his familiar tropes are permitted a final moving permutation:

My tumor is not interested in love,
no neoplasm is – the blind cells thereof
are not interested in love or affection,
she sends out little colonies, chipped genes
mark their crossing the river, they are
without variation, they keep time with terror.

W.N. Herbert

*Bleeding Edge*. Jonathan Cape. ISBN 9780224099028. HBK. £20
Thomas Pynchon

Less than two weeks after the destruction of the World Trade Centre, *Time Magazine* published an article by Roger Rosenblatt entitled 'The Age of Irony Comes to an End':

> One good thing could come from this horror: it could spell the *end of the age of irony*. For some 30 years – roughly as long as the Twin Towers were upright – the good folks in charge of America's intellectual life have insisted that nothing was to be believed in or taken seriously. Nothing was real.... The ironists, seeing through everything, made it difficult for anyone to see anything. The consequences of thinking that nothing is real – apart from prancing around in an air of vain stupidity – is that one will not know the difference between a joke and a menace. No more. The planes that plowed into the World Trade Center and the Pentagon were real. The flames, smoke sirens – real. The chalky landscape, the silence of the streets – all real.

Even if they weren't directly enabled by the loss of reality in the postmodern 'age of irony', the terrorist strikes, Rosenblatt argues, brutally reinstated the need for hard distinctions between fact and fiction, fantasy and truth. A new realism was required. After the attacks, no sensible person could have any truck with the whimsy, uncertainty and ontological game-playing that had become so fashionable in literature and culture over the past decades. No principled writer could possibly return to the postmodern mischief of the pre-9/11 world, and they certainly couldn't presume to depict the events of that day in a manner that refused to spell out clearly 'the difference between a joke and a menace'. Could they?

*Bleeding Edge*, the most recent novel by Thomas Pynchon – presumably one of the 'good folks in charge of America's intellectual life' targeted by Rosenblatt's piece – does just this. The novel's depiction of 9/11, which takes place two thirds of the way through and breaks traumatically into the characters' world, transforming the tone of the narrative entirely, is ironically anticipated by, projected through and depicted in terms of all of the paranoid conspiracy theories that did the rounds at the time, and takes as read in its complex and convoluted narrative the impossibility of stepping outside of such fantasies to identify a clearly defined political reality and explanation. Fantasy and fact, the virtual and the real, menace and hilarity are all interwoven in the narrative's texture. Moreover, at a key moment the novel responds explicitly to Rosenblatt's accusation, projecting it back at the reader. Soon after the event, the protagonist's sister confronts her over dinner:

> 'Whose side are you on, are you American or what are you?' Brooke now in full indignation, 'this horrible, horrible tragedy, a whole generation traumatised, war with the Arab world any minute, and even this isn't safe from your stupid little hipster irony? What next, Auschwitz jokes?' (324)

As readers of a text focalised entirely through the eyes of the protagonist, we have shared her views and experiences of people and events throughout, and cannot escape being implicated ourselves as this accusation is levelled at her. And that, perhaps, is a key point the novel makes...

The plot and narrative of *Bleeding Edge* are slightly more straightforward than those found in much of Pynchon's earlier work. In terms of time and space, rather than spanning centuries and continents as novels such as *The Crying of Lot 49*, *V.*, and *Against the Day* all do, it focuses on just a year (between the bursting of the dotcom bubble and the Spring of 2002) and a single place: the state of New York, Manhattan Island in particular. The story follows Maxine Tarnow, an independent financial fraud investigator, as she looks into hashslingerz, a company that has not just survived the dotcom crash but seems to have profited massively from it, and its elusive and menacing CEO Gabriel Ice – a man who 'makes Bill Gates look charismatic' (11). As with Pynchon's other detective-genre writing, *Lot 49* and *Inherent Vice* in particular, what begins as a relatively contained and coherent investigation (execute a will, track down a missing lover) soon spirals out of the protagonist's control to take in a vast array of characters, plots, secrets and bizarre cultural ephemera. In this case, Maxine's investigation of hashslingerz's accounts finds myriad links with the likes of New York real-estate agents, members of the US security services, Mossad, Middle-Eastern terrorist and counter-terrorist organisations, Russian gangsters, and the computer companies, innovators and freelancers that are going over the traces of the dotcom failures to gain control of the future of the internet.

Absolute distinctions between reality and the virtuality of cyberspace are frequently questioned as Maxine's investigation ventures further into the mysterious and unregulated 'deep web' that remains beyond commercial control and is the province of computer geeks, criminals, government agents, and other invaders and refugees from the day-to-day world, as well as, possibly, the ghosts of those killed by terrorists or the state. Such 'ontological uncertainty' (as Brian McHale, one of Pynchon's most influential critics, describes it) and the paranoia it produces is entirely typical of Pynchon's work, though the virtual / real of *Bleeding Edge* is probably closer to the opposition structuring *Inherent Vice* between sober and stoned visions of reality than the vertiginous collapsing of paranoia, fantasy, dream, intoxication and madness that makes any certainty about reality in a novel such as *Gravity's Rainbow* impossible. And this uncertainty is a key part of the fun.

*Bleeding Edge* also displays the sort of brilliant and bizarre humour for which Pynchon is known. Among the vast array of exquisitely sketched characters, there are such creations as Reg Despard whose inept attempts to pirate movies with an early hand-held camera are discovered by an NYU film professor to stand at 'the leading edge of this post-postmodern art form' with their 'neo-Brechtian subversion of diegesis' (9), Felix Boïngueaux who sports 'a strange do, which is either a triple-digit power haircut… or else he cut it himself and fucked it up' (151), and Lester Conkling who is a 'freelance professional Nose' (201) who uses his ultra-refined sense of smell to solve crimes as he obsessively searches for a sample of Hitler's cologne. There are also the appalling puns (a strip club called 'Joie de Beavre', for example), witty vignettes (an episode where a brash yuppie jumps the queue at Thanksgiving, is knocked unconscious by a flung frozen turkey and carefully stepped on by all those he pushed ahead of) and weird speculations (time travel sponsored by the CIA is mooted at one point). Packed into less than 500 pages, the pace never lets up.

In the end, there is no resolution to the plots, paranoid speculations and ontological uncertainties: no final truth about the extent to which hashslingerz, Gabriel Ice, the CIA, Mossad, the Mafia and the numerous other potential villains are implicated in the terrorist attacks comes to light. Instead, clinging on to irony, *Bleeding Edge* rejects the '"reality" programming [that] is suddenly all over cable, like dog shit' (and, in fact has an increasingly absurd and hilarious running joke at their expense) and refuses to be 'freed from the fictions that led [us] so astray, as if paying attention to made-up lives was some form of *evil drug abuse* that the collapse of the towers cured by scaring everybody straight again' (335). Among its many brilliant ideas, insights and images, one commitment the novel retains is to the power of imaginative fiction to resist the totalitarian violence of both terror and the war against it.

Simon Malpas

*The Hotel Oneira.* Faber. ISBN 9780571305599. £12.99
August Kleinzahler

'This 9-room house could be the home of your dreams', ran the online real estate advert for 83 Bluff Road, Fort Lee, New Jersey in the autumn of 2009. Looking closely at the accompanying photographs – still available for the curious Googler to peruse on the real estate website – you can make out, in the threshold of a doorway, the figure of August Kleinzahler slightly out of focus as he is captured on the move from one room to another. The atmospheric setting of such earlier poems as 'Before Dawn on Bluff Road' and 'Gray Light in May' (among many others), 83 Bluff Road is the house in which Kleinzahler grew up and to which, from his rented apartment in San Francisco, he has been returning since the age of seventeen, as he described in an intimate diary account of the trauma of 'selling up' published in the *LRB* some months after the sale closed:

> This is home, even if I haven't really lived here for 42 years, my psychological redoubt: red brick, slate-roofed, sitting on a 500-foot basalt sill that reaches down to the 'lordly Hudson'. It is what is most solid about me and what has allowed me to live the sort of life one might not associate with any notion of solidity. This is who I am, what I'm from. And with the sale of the house goes my connection to this place. I am untethered.

Describing himself in a *Guardian* interview as a 'kindred spirit to the Chinese poets of the Tang dynasty who write about being cast into exile in the western mountains', Kleinzahler identified himself on his visits home as 'separate enough as a formed adult to distance myself, while at the same time very much caught up in the gravitational fields of memory and sensation, the eerily persistent emotions of long ago.' And so we discover him now in the poems of *The Hotel Oneira*, among exiles, having finally, it would seem, left home for good at the appropriately autumnal age of sixty.

Of course he has only left home in one sense. Though now, in reality, home to a young Chinese couple, the house at 83 Bluff Road has indeed become the home of Kleinzahler's dreams, imaginatively upgraded into the roomier and more variously populated Hotel Oneira; the opening poem of the collection locates the poet-as-dreamer, 'settled in again by the Hudson at the Hotel Oneira: / maps on the walls, shelves of blue and white Pelicans' wherein one can 'feel the rumble of the trains / vibrating up the steel of the hotel's frame.' Nothing exists apart from the poet's imagination: 'I can feel it inside my head', he writes of the emotional freight that is being shifted: 'What is in those railcars is also inside my head'. If the title reminds many readers of John Ashbery's *Hotel Lautréamont* that seems fitting, particularly when we remember Ashbery's own feelings about hotels: 'There is something very attractive about a hotel because it has got so many rooms, and so many different kinds of people all doing different things.' It is a hotel of the mind and (to borrow another tell-tale phrase from Kleinzahler's *LRB* diary) one that has no end of 'memory-driven emotional weather blowing through' it. Given how Kleinzahler, as Fort Lee's poet laureate, is duty-bound to celebrate his home-town as the 'birthplace of American film', a filmic analogy seems called for here and, for me, reading *The Hotel Oneira* is akin to being hauled through the 2010 film *Inception* locked in the multi-level dream expanses of the characters' subconscious imaginations. Walking the sumptuously decorated hotel corridors of Kleinzahler's subconscious makes for an equally unsettling and no less exhilarating experience.

Not surprisingly, the residents of the Hotel Oneira are an eclectic mix: exiles, ghosts (of former lovers, family members) and other revenants and passers-through flit between floors. Of the poetic presiding spirits, T.S. Eliot (along with Lee Harwood, James Schuyler and Vachel Lindsay, among others) comes and goes, while Basil Bunting overhears all from his penthouse suite and in-house lawyer Wallace Stevens reminds guests at check-in that 'we live in a place / That is not our own and, much more, not ourselves'. 'A Wine Tale', dedicated to Lee Harwood, summons to mind the ghost of Yeats's 'All Soul's Night' (that 'sharpened by death [...] drinks from the wine breath') and Kleinzahler's description of Harwood's work – 'poetry that approximates the strange or extreme dislocations and transitions of dream life' – is true of Kleinzahler's own shadowy poetic movements throughout. Of Ashbery's distinctive aesthetic strategies, Kleinzahler appreciatively has noted how, 'The thing to watch for, his best trick, is the insertion of something poignant amid the dizzying spectacle, thus sandbagging the reader.' That Kleinzahler is drawn to both Ashbery and Harwood as model poets of 'atmosphere, but atmosphere disrupted' is no surprise and both are VIP guests at the Hotel Oneira.

Drawn as he is to cultural collisions, European composers and artists who fled fascism in Europe for America (many of whom, including Theodor Adorno and Arnold Schoenberg, settled in California) in the 1930s and 40s can be made out through the hotel windows: 'Rose Exile', a bizarre parade of European-exported Americana features Adorno and Ethel Merman at loggerheads while 'Exiles' takes as its atonal sounding board émigré composer Krenek's description of the 'echolessness of the vast American expanses'. The incongruity of (a fictive) Nietzsche in Bel-Air (in 'Exiles') brings to mind the famous footage of George Gershwin and Arnold Schoenberg playing tennis in Hollywood. Elsewhere, in 'Rain', we look in on Francis Ponge enjoying *Looney Tunes, Vols I. and II* on a loop. As Adorno's artistic legacy in 'Rose Exile' is reduced to a writing desk on a Pasadena parade float, famous lines from his *Minima Moralia* seem most apt here in a collection that is most of all a sustained, elegiac flight around ideas of imaginative home and homelessness, self-estrangement and the beguiling strangeness of words: 'For a man who no longer has a homeland, writing becomes a place to live […] In the end, the writer is not even allowed to live in his writing.' Ghosts from closer to 'home' also feature; it may be the ghost of Kleinzahler's brother Harris (the subject of his 2005 memoir *Cutty, One Rock*) that is addressed in 'The Crossing', the poem doubling as both an elegy to a beloved companion who departed the world on his own terms and a meditation on the poetic act as one of endless translation and metaphor-making in the 'shadow country', the interstices between zones. After all, in the words of Chris Whitley, the itinerant song-writer quoted by Kleinzahler in the same memoir: 'Home is where you come across'.

Places have always been for Kleinzahler 'conditions of mind', his multi-layered poetic mind most 'hyper-awake' (to use his phrase) when most displaced, dislocated, as he has outlined in *Cutty, One Rock*, focusing on the 'window' that presents itself 'after travelling by air between places, places where you've lived for a long time' inside of which usually too-familiar features of the landscape (buildings, river light) 'become almost stereoscopic, carrying a taste of the unreal – as if the world had been passed through a solution, cleansed.' It helps to enter the Hotel Oneira through such a window. So many of these poems begin to form themselves during those strange hours that travellers (and poets) keep: 'pre-dawn', 'at 3.a.m.', 'before dawn' and 'in the depths of night' being the timescapes throughout. The 'condition of mind' in which words come tentatively, elusively, through the fog, the scrim, is movingly felt across the line-break spaces in the 'Wind/Work' section of 'Summer Journal':

> I lie there struggling to remember a word.
> It takes a while

> but it's not far. As I begin to doze off
> it comes to me,
> as so many things do in this condition of mind.

A self-appointed 'fog-chaser', Kleinzahler's poetic mind is the most sensitive of musical and meteorological instruments laying itself open to the pressures of the elements; the poet himself makes no secret of valuing rain and fog most of all for the way that they form 'another layer between [poet] and the world' in which 'light is softer, sounds are muffled'. Kleinzahler, as atmographer and diarist of Edgewater, New Jersey, surely identifies with Thomas Appletree, whose weather diaries he self-delightingly plunders for his poem 'The Exquisite Atmography of Thomas Appletree, Diarist of Edgiock', an opulent, symphonic performance of meteorological forces in harmony and disarray. Fittingly for a music critic and collector, the *Hotel*'s ambient music is an unpredictable soundtrack that ranges from seventeenth-century composers Biber and Schmeltzer to Richard Wagner, Whitney Houston and be-bop. Kleinzahler's avowed bid to 'capture the physical world through the sound and movement of language' comes off throughout so many of these linguistically sumptuous poems, as in the 'ominous strange music' of the lavish fantasia 'When the Barocco'. Continually testing and tasting words, his 'Cabinet of Timbres' (as another section of 'Summer Journal' terms it) is copious in the extreme and readers expecting the poet's trademark variety of veering tonalities and clashing registers will not be left wanting. As he wrote in a more recent poem to his teacher Basil Bunting: 'You poured those sounds [Scarlatti, Dowland, Byrd, Wordsworth, Wyatt] into our heads. / Who knew what might come of it?'. Kleinzahler's adventures in music continue with unstoppable force. Indeed, a line from his review of Roy Fisher seems an apt description of his own poetry in this collection more than anywhere else: ' You don't know where you are or who's on board. The metamorphoses are tonal, and proceed glacially, like the massive tone clusters of a Ligeti orchestral piece.'

The collection ends in unknown waters with the poem 'Traveler's Tales: Chapter 12', as a cruise ship heads off in the direction of Point Blanco – the exact location of which remains, to this reader at least, unclear. Even Google maps draws a blank, which may be exactly the point; Kleinzahler's mapmaking is entirely his own. Wherever on earth we find ourselves at collection's end, we find the poet-as-traveller revisiting an old friend from his Vancouver days, pronouncing on matters to do with friendship after a long life and open, as ever, to further adventures. 'I love coming to New Jersey, but I love missing it, too', Kleinzahler opined in an interview for the *Guardian* in 2009. One may wonder where the work will come from now that 83 Bluff Road, the 'centre of his being' as he has described it, has been passed into the hands of other occupants but one need not worry that such an earthly loss will deter the endless imaginative inventions and weathered artistic sensitivities of such a thrilling, uniquely-tuned poetic mind in its meanderings and endless modulations.

Maria Johnston

*Go Giants*. Faber. ISBN 9780571288182. £12.99
Nick Laird

Pick up a new poetry collection next time you're in your local indie bookshop and, chances are, on the dust jacket, you'll find the usual publisher's puff. You know the kind of thing: a smart but predictable blurb extolling the brilliance of the poems therein, or else a few quotes from reviews and contemporaries. Should you happen on Nick Laird's third book of poems, *Go Giants*, though, you'll spot something else – a freewheeling paean that (and I say this at the happy risk of furnishing Faber with an endorsement to pin on Laird's follow-up) is up there with the best hymns to poetry you'll come across. Making a mockery of those who reckon the living art form 'a joke; outmoded as the nose flute' or else 'a pimped-out souped-up pussy-magnet', i.e. just the kind of X Factor-type fuckwittery that would put poetry 'to a phone-in vote', this title-less prologue conjures a personal reminiscence that stops you in your tracks. Here we find poetry 'mooching round the back of the loading dock at the meat factory', a kind of 'sympathetic magic' at odds with the machinations of profit and want; a juncture, as Laird fancies it, 'of the two kinds of real, the act caught in the act'. 'And if it so happens that you are the flawed compensation for our having just the one go', our poet concludes, 'it does for me, or very nearly'.

It's smart stuff, this subverting of the space where you'd expect to find banal marketing journalese. And not just because the verve and flair of the writing here gets us onside, even before we reach the book's first poem proper. Ironically enough, it also serves as a précis of what's to come. Since his lauded first collection, *To a Fault* (2005), and its swift follow-up *On Purpose* (2007), Laird's poetry has combined edgy vernacular, blunt reportage, and an increasingly scientific materialist cast of mind that can border on the grandiose. His aesthetic seems to be one that foregrounds acute contemplation – the act of poetry – as the only means of getting at the world's real nature; beyond what one poem, 'Envy', calls 'the hot pennies of unhappiness' inherent to being human, in the hope of finding 'something like the freedom of the universe'. Extending his engagement with the fault lines between his abiding themes – the personal and political, home and flight, religion and secularity, intimacy and violence – *Go Giants* documents a struggle, one in which Laird looks to push his poems into unexpected, often playful directions.

'You're beeswax and I'm birdshit', trills the first line of opener 'Epithalamium'. A serio-comic tribute to marriage and the idea that opposites attract, it also reads as a manifesto – here is poetry as a blurring and transformation of the seemingly irreconcilable into one: 'and I am Trafalgar, and you're Waterloo, / and frequently it seems to me that I am you, / and you are me.' But this isn't Raymond Chandler's mock exasperation at the fact that, for writers, everything has to be like something else. It's more a metaphysical recognition that the poet's job (if he or she has one) is to uncover the interconnectedness of things. Just as 'Condolence' develops a childhood memory of the poet's mother composing letters by the fire into an image that speaks of wider Troubles-era grief and collapse (brought up in County Tyrone, Laird is a son of Northern Ireland's fraught political conflicts), the title poem pastes together pop culture phrases, clichés and surreal imperatives into a dislocated commentary on our frenetic modern lives. The two are radically different poems – one a touching familial recollection; the other, a set of disembodied marching orders – but both are attempts to connect with a primal sense of absolute unity. Suspicious of religious faith but, by his own admission, drawn to its trappings, *Go Giants* finds Laird repeatedly turning to a mix of poetry and scientific hard-thinking in the hope of supplanting the religions – specifically Christianity – he, like most of us, have fallen away from, but are still to find the desired replacement for. 'To see the gods withdraw, / dethroned, exposed to ridicule, / was our allotted truth' he writes with resignation in 'The Effects'; 'they weren't dislodged / by other, stronger gods: / they simply came to nothing. / That line of enquiry closed.' One of the book's best poems, it ends on an image of a mongrel dog 'running / masterless' among a congregation 'mid-hymn'. Poetry can be like this, it seems to say – playful, life-affirming, eye-opening, and something to which our 'faces turn, / one-by-one and radiant'.

It is this blend of earnest and buoyant ambition with intelligence, feeling and a genuine sense of fun that makes Laird's poetry so readable. Even when sound and sense divide to leave the writing more than a little prosaic, Laird packs in enough, and is so questing and entertainingly inquisitive in his frames of reference, you can't help but forgive it. 'Progress', a fragmented bildungsroman of a sequence that closes the book, draws on Galileo, Pope Urban the Eighth, The Smiths, the art of pint-pulling and the persisting sectarianism of the Troubles – a feat in itself. But it is in the quieter lyrics, finding consolation in the comforts of our domestic lives, that his talent really shines. 'Talking in Kitchens' is a beautiful vignette to love and companionship, in a world where 'nobody knows how we feel and it's fine'. Its final couplet is one of the most moving and *echt* I've read in years, and fully earned: 'Here it is written down if I forget to say it – / my home is the temple made by your hands.'

As a title, *Go Giants* straightforwardly reads as a cultural reference to the eponymous American football team, on the US's East Coast where Laird increasingly spends his time. It also looks like a mischievous dismissal of those Ulster poets – Yeats, Mahon, Heaney – that have exerted influence on his writing from the get-go. But more fully than either of those, it is a clarion call for poetry to up its game; to be more than a trifling art form, but something we can all find solace, excitement, surprise and truth in. He mightn't always hit the mark, but Laird deserves credit for this ambitious and entertaining book. God willing, it should find a decent audience too.

Ben Wilkinson

*Tenth of December.* Bloomsbury Publishing. ISBN 9781408837368. £8.99
George Saunders

Want to catch up on the current state of American fiction? It could take time. A brief glance through end-of-year critics' lists yields few novels that come in at under 500 pages. Donna Tartt's *The Goldfinch*? 784 pages. Dave Eggers' *The Circle*? 504. All of which makes Thomas Pynchon's *The Bleeding Edge* (weighing in at a mere 496) feel downright slender. Is it possible to read a work of contemporary fiction without incurring a wrist injury?

Happily, the answer is yes.

Look no further than George Saunders' brilliant new collection, *Tenth of December*. Saunders has been dazzling readers with his biting satire and dark humour for decades, but this new collection is his best. While his acclaimed 'CivilWarLand in Bad Decline' is a masterpiece of short fiction, the collection that bears its name (1996) is somewhat uneven. Likewise, *Pastoralia* (1999) and *In Persuasion Nation* (2007) feel more like stories-written-during-a-certain-time-period gathered between two covers, rather than carefully orchestrated collections. Not so the *Tenth of December*. These stories fizz with the verve and wild originality that characterise Saunders' short fiction, but when read alongside one another, they reverberate and clash, creating dissonant chords and blistering harmonies that resonate long after one has set the book aside.

Take 'Sticks', which I first encountered back in 1994 when it appeared in *STORY* magazine. It has finally found a home as the second story in this collection and could not be better placed. After the suffocating interiority of 'Victory Lap' ('Scary! Kissing Matt was like suddenly this cow in a sweater is bearing down on you, who will not take no for an answer, and his huge cow head is being flooded by chemicals that are drowning out what little powers of reason Matt actually did have.' p. 7), the stylistic rigour of 'Sticks' has an almost liberating effect in retrospect. 'Sticks' is story of one man's life distilled into two paragraphs, and its terse lyricism comes like a much needed lungful of oxygen after the emotional maelstrom of 'Victory Lap'. But the respite is brief, for in the story that follows, ('Puppy'), the pummelling resumes with wave after wave of claustrophobic interior monologue.

From here, we are hurled into the emotional intensity of 'Escape from Spiderhead' where violent criminals serve as human guinea pigs in drug trials. Our narrator's emotions are dictated by a MobiPak TM affixed to his body that delivers pharmaceuticals to make him more articulate (Verbaluce TM) truthful (VeriTalk TM), obedient (Docilryde TM), or suicidal (Darkenfloxx

TM), depending on what buttons his captor/scientist presses in his remote control. 'Escape from Spiderhead' contains all the imaginative verve, originality, and technical wizardry for which Saunders has become famous, yet without a whiff of cruelty. Lately, critics have begun to call attention to the strain of tenderness in Saunders' work – to his sharp, yet compassionate eye – a quality that backlights the satire of 'Home'.

'Home' chronicles the misadventures of Mikey, an army vet recently discharged under dubious circumstances, as he struggles to navigate a homefront full of people eager to assault him with their gratitude ('thank you for your service!') as a kind of inoculation against any real knowledge of what they might be thanking him for: 'My cousin's there. At one of them. At least I think he is. He was supposed to go. We were never that close.' (p. 184). Saunders's satire cuts deep. But the knife he wields is that of a surgeon, not a butcher. He is not out to dissect the rotting corpse of America, but to slice out its tumourous growths and force us to confront every ugly, fatal contour, in the hope, however faint, of remission.

The disease? In Saunders' work the cancer eating away at America is capitalism – consumerism in all its absurd, sinister, laughable, morally dubious and deadly guises. I have yet to encounter a more devastating dramatisation of the subtle insidiousness of American capitalism than 'Semplica Girl Diaries'. This story plunges us into the life of a hapless father who spends his days toiling away as a middle management schlub in order to provide for his family, a narrative delivered through diary entries that pelt us with the raw data of his days: 'Will write twenty minutes a night, no matter how tired. So goodnight to all future generations. Please know I was a person like you, I too breathed air and tensed legs while trying to sleep and, when writing with pencil, sometimes brought pencil to nose to smell' (p. 110). Our narrator is a goof, but a loveable one, whose daily struggles are rendered in jagged sentence fragments that capture the emotional whirr of contemporary life: 'Stood looking up at house, sad. Thought: why sad? Don't be sad. If sad, will make everyone sad. Went in happy, not mentioning broken bumper, squirrel/mouse smudge, maggots, then gave Eva extra ice cream as had spoken harshly to her. … Have to do better! Be kinder. Start now. Soon they will be grown and how sad, if only memory is of testy stressed guy in bad car' (p. 112). Slowly, however, readers piece together a horrifying fact: our narrator's class anxieties have led him to decorate his yard with SGs, a euphemism for Semplica Girls. These are women from third-world countries who earn residence visas by having a microline strung through their brains (painlessly) then get strung aloft to serve as lawn decorations for wealthy suburbanites. And yet, despite our horror as this fact dawns, Saunders has enmeshed us so deeply in the narrator's psyche that we cannot stop sympathising with his plight as a struggling, misguided father. His action is morally reprehensible, yet still we root for him as he begs his wife's father for a loan, feeling pained and ashamed for him as we read his father-in-law's devastating, judgemental refusal.

Sanders' fiction is often dubbed Orwellian or Pynchonesque, but the writer that *Tenth of December* brings most forcefully to mind is Barry Hannah. Like Hannah's best work, these stories explore a region of America that no other writer has attempted to survey. But it is not a region you will find on a map. Saunders' country is a global capitalist nowheresville that feels at once familiar yet grotesque – a place peopled by men in dead-end, vaguely humiliating jobs, by mothers in Target jeans struggling to endure demanding kids. They work in half-finished strip malls in Exurbia or theme parks gone to seed, struggling to communicate in a slack vernacular that has corroded their moral sense and made them prey to forces beyond their ken. And yet… they are still people. And the acerbic tenderness with which Saunders renders their plight will leave you, at the end of 251 pages, longing for more.

Allyson Stack

*Pilgrim's Flower*. Picador. ISBN 97814472-42178. PBK. £9.99
Rachael Boast

With its yearning for retreat and church visits, Rachael Boast's *Pilgrim's Flower* provides a sequel to her award-winning debut, *Sidereal* (2011). Both books are in two parts, suggesting a structural fidelity, and while Boast's first book was governed by constellations, Scottish locations, and lonely journeys, her religious interest lamenting what is 'holy/ but is perhaps diseased' (as she wrote in 'Blind Date'), this new work is a series of pilgrimages across Scotland and England to abbeys, rivers, landscapes, forgotten back lanes, and gardens. There are literary rewrites, references and epigraphs – Robert Lowell, Anna Ahkmatova, Jean Cocteau, Coleridge, Brodsky, Rimbaud, Ciaran Carson, Sappho – but the tone is similar to fellow Picador poet Katharine Towers, and the style is more influenced by 1990s Seamus Heaney, by *Seeing Things* and *The Spirit Level* (scribes and saints, hope for epiphany, tercets reminiscent of 'Squarings') and by Don Paterson (sonnets with liminal spaces, shores, Antonio Macado). Boast's subjects are largely free of the twenty-first century, and each gaze outwards leads to lyrical introspection, love, loneliness, and an unnamed 'you'.

The ten-poem sequence 'Anon' crystallises the book's themes, interested in the freedom of anonymity that is conferred by quiet wandering, 'Walking the tributaries that weave between/ the old wool villages, their wash-stones,/ well-heads and babble ongoing'. The poem acknowledges an 'urge for the uncivil, for farm track/ and furrow', and in its retreat into nowhere, sound and perspective grow clear: 'A rooftop settlement, green moss basks in its conquests/ and private concerns'. In 'The Garden Path', growth in the British mammal population is discovered by the river, 'a low ebb for paw prints/ in the silt of the bank,/ otter or mink'. But lines like 'The river knows how to keep going' exemplify how cliché and hackneyed phrase lessen the impact of *Pilgrim's Flower*.

In his poem 'Workshop Dream', novelist-cum-stand-up-poet Joe Dunthorne adapted the use of cliché in mainstream poetry in order to satirise it: 'We stepped out onto the beach. The water/ made the sound: cliché, cliché, cliché'. He did so within a mainstream context influenced by Luke Kennard, but his adaptation made a virtue of the poetic strategies he was satirising. It is an interesting counterpoint to *Pilgrim's Flower*, where the central problem is twofold: firstly, if the clichéd phrases were deleted ('how all things are cut/ from the same rock', 'going just according to plan', 'the power of love', 'the universal truth', 'to wander off the track'), it would not harm the sense or meaning of the poems; secondly, because of the tendency, or habit, to lean toward tidy epiphany through the use of cliché, the original idea of the poem is cut short, denied development, short-circuited.

It is this twofold problem which dogs 'To St Mary Redcliffe', a pilgrimage into a 12th century church in Bristol, which is home to a Chaotic Pendulum, a hollow metal beam filled with recycled water which tips the weight unpredictably left or right, giving chaotic permutations of movement. The details, or problems, of how it works are omitted from the poem itself, which digresses into the church and its environs, 'the route gets complex,/ and I'm diverted around toxic investments/ and half-built car parks'. The pendulum is described as 'a miracle of rare device', but there is no investigation of it *as a cross* on a Christian altar, to provoke ideas of this religious poet's faith and its oscillations. There could be relevance in terms of Chaos Theory, or, it could have provided a 'metaphysic(al) challenge' (to adapt a phrase from the book's blurb), via John Donne's 'A Nocturnal upon St Lucy's Day, Being the Shortest Day': 'Oft a flood / Have we two wept, and so / Drowned the whole world, us two; oft did we grow / To be two chaoses'. But the conceit is stopped abruptly.

'Songs (After Macado)' is not so much a version poem '(After Macado)' but rather ('After Macado, After Don Paterson)'. This poem is a rewrite from part VII of Antonio Macado's 'Other Songs for Guiomar', out of which Paterson made a sonnet called 'Poetry', and which Boast has now rewritten as 'Songs'. Where the diamond of the original poem metaphorically holds the earth's fire, which Paterson writes as the 'bright coal of his love', Boast inverts the diamond-as-elemental energy-and-love idea in favour of real burning coal: 'there's little love in a diamond;/ better the bright coal whose heat/ forces it apart into a hundred fires'. This is a new take on the analogy, but the overall strategy is the same as Paterson's, but she repeats Paterson's phrase 'oblivious sky' at the close, and the whole method is identical to Paterson's, one which he developed across his versions of Macado in *The Eyes* (Faber, 1999). In the context of *Pilgrim's Flower*, Macado's sonnet II, 'Pilgrim, a wonder awaits you on the road', might have provided an alternative route for rewriting.

Published just two years after her debut, a slower process of revision may have made the material stronger, to open a freer dialogue with Boast's influences, and with the subjects of the poems.

Simon Pomery

*The Dead Zoo*. The Gallery Press. ISBN 978 1 85235 568 5. PBK. £10.50
Ciaran Berry

> *Under a framed photograph of Hong Kong*
> *The proprietor of the Chinese restaurant*
> *Stands at the door as if the world were young,*
> *Watching the first yacht hoist a sail*
> —Derek Mahon, from 'The Chinese Restaurant in Portrush'

In the mid-18th century a group of Irish-language poets, the *Fili na Maighe* (Poets of the Maigue), held meetings in Croom, Co. Cork. They took their name from the river that runs beside the pub, and the pub, in turn, came to be known as The Poet's Corner. Today the building houses a Chinese restaurant. This lends itself, if only metaphorically, to my untested theory that the appearance of Mahon's Chinese restaurant marks a turning point in contemporary Irish poetry; the moment when the supremacy of Celtic symbolism begins to give way to an international advance. While it might have some distance to go before it replaces swans, it is remarkable how often the Chinese restaurant appears in the contemporary poetic landscape, perhaps most strikingly deployed by Conor O'Callaghan – for whom Mahon is an important influence – as well as in the work of, amongst others, Kevin Higgins, Gerard Smyth, and now Ciaran Berry:

> caught as we were on the far side of the border
> in a seaside town at the dead of winter,
>     across from the battened down funfair
>     and the boarded up arcades between
> a barbershop and Chinese Takeaway, where
> the carp would soon be floating on their sides.

This passage, from 'On the Jukebox of the Morning After the Night Before', nods to both Mahon and O'Callaghan (see the latter's 'East' and 'Seatown') but if Mahon's poem is an awakening, 'as if the world was young', Berry's poem, and indeed much of this collection, is a closing down, a winding up of song. Here, he recalls a friendship that was once vibrant and defined in part by music, but one that 'would always be the words / of a dead man or a dead woman locked / in the circumlocutions of melody'.

But it isn't only the carp that are in the process of dying; so are Berry's relatives and friends, memory, and the Earth itself. These, in effect, stand shoulder-to-shoulder with the preserved animals of Dublin's Natural History Museum (the eponymous Dead Zoo) and are joined by Berry's numerous historical figures (most prominently Darwin, Einstein and Augustine but also Nero, Fanny Alexander, Whitman, Jemmy Button, Alzheimer, *et al*), mythological heroes, a Japanese ghost ship, and old films and photographs. They are all '"Ghost figures, I want to say, or 'bees in amber"' ('Schoolchildren, Cashelnagore'). Several of the strongest poems are delicate, disguised elegies – 'Spooky Action at a Distance' and 'Elephants on the Black Strand', for instance – and I use the word 'disguised' because these are not eulogies that simply highlight the deceased's positive traits. Instead, while the subjects' deaths are painful for the author, their passing is one part of a greater picture.

As is typical of Berry's compositional process, in these elegies he combines seemingly disparate images so that it is not until the penny drops, and the entirety of the thought process is revealed, that we appreciate both the full intent and full impact of the poem. In 'Spooky Action at a Distance', for a cousin who 'will always be a girl in jodhpurs', we are treated to a space in which '[t]he past, the future were entangled particles'; where particles of horses and greyhounds, Einstein, Brahms, psychokinetic twins, old cars, and rotting fruit, entwine until will return once again to Einstein, alone on a sea voyage:

> swaying so that his pen rolls back and forth
>    across his midnight desk, his insignificance
> and ours has never been more apparent,
> yet all he can do is smile, far from anyone
>    and well beyond caring, and for once I envy him
> such indifference.

Our miniscule place in the universe has been confirmed, but so, too, has the wonder of human achievement and, crucially, the value of the one precious life that has been lost. It is a remarkable accomplishment, and the level of this accomplishment is repeated time and again.

As these elegies prove, if the collection has death as a central theme, the possibility of salvation is of equal importance – in the humanist rather than religious sense, derived from our interconnectedness: 'how every body becomes the body of another / and how, in this there is the only real order" ('The Exhibition of the Bodies'). This is the wonder of existence; the counterpoint to death. The conjuring of wonder is the subject of 'At Ballyconneely', where an entire Connemara village is said to have witnessed a mirage on the horizon. It is there, too, in what is conjured from the silence of John Cage's silent composition ('4′ 33″'). The productive condition of 'silence' is championed throughout the collection and is the devotional state that Berry repeatedly demands for the appreciation of the physical world. In a sequence of 16-line poems, speaking as Fanny Alexander who wrote the hymn 'All Things Bright and Beautiful', he suggests that 'each letter becomes a sort of cypher', and one suspects his own almost spiritual devotion to the composition process.

The final, apocalyptic poem 'Snipers, Anthrax, Dead Racoons', *The Dead Zoo*'s final poem, offers one of the bleakest appraisals of the Earth's health that you are likely to encounter. Again uniting disparate elements, Berry leaves us in a post 9/11 world where Cerberus-like rottweilers and inhuman acts of terrorism thrive in 'the year / after the dust of human bones floated over / the East River'. The dust mirrors the collection's often referenced snow which, here, is sinisterly omnipresent: 'like snow, the news came slow at first'; 'I see it [snow] settling down around the boles / of half-bare trees'; '"eath having fallen like snow / from envelopes with no return address'. The concluding image is of a dead racoon, the river's flotsam and final exhibit of the Dead Zoo, 'rotting on the lawn, for crying / out loud, and the air reeked still of burning'. The enjambment complicates and rejuvenates the fixed expression, illustrating Berry's awareness of the implications inherent in formal decisions.

Take, as another example, how a poem's subject is served best by either division into regular stanzas or contained within weightier blocks of writing. As an example of the later, in 'Connemara Donkeys' the monotony of these creatures' lives (these '[m]igrant workers') is reflected in an uninterrupted litany of the narrator's confined journeys through landscapes, employing long sentences that push relentlessly forward, until we reach the desolate final image:

> [...] all through
> that year bald tyres rode the suddenly singed air,
> so that, even now, somewhere glass shatters
> and the view becomes more clear: this life goes by
> on hooves, a swarm of flies about its bloodshot eyes.

In contrast, 'The Irish Sheep Boy' is concerned, in part, with the awkwardness of a wild boy's body being prepared for display. The repeated use of enjambment between the three-line stanzas neatly mirrors the difficulty of twisting the poor wretch into some recognisably human form, each stanza being a broken step toward the ghoulish objective:

> consider him, head down, the one black sheep
>
> in the flock that dots the hill's incline, the wind-scoured
> precipice of a sea cliff, where his gnarled teeth
> picked between clover and vetch – this boy brought live
>
> across the dykes and fens into this frigid room,

In this passage, too, we have evidence of Berry's natural ear for rhythms as well as assonantal and alliterative effects: 'in the flock that dots the hill's incline', and "across the dykes and fens into this frigid room'. But, as you will hopefully discover for yourselves, the craft is everywhere.

It is easy to read 'The Irish Sheep Boy' as a direct descendant of Heaney's bog-body poems. On the day that Heaney died, one commentator wrote that we are now on our own and although I appreciate the intensity of emotion that elicited the sentiment, surely we are left with the great man's poetry and therefore can never be on our own, literarily. As writers and readers we are interconnected, and the perpetuating nature of this continuum is something to be valued. Perhaps this is the greatest strength of Berry's collection: it confirms not only our losses but also our shared worth. So, to end where we began, by way of metaphor: the Chinese takeaway in Croom was recently trashed by yobs. The villagers were so appalled by the violation that they banded together to support the business. With the community's help the proprietor now 'stands at the door again'. The Poets' Corner is once more open for business.

Paul Maddern

*Echo's Grove: Collected Translations.* The Gallery Press. HBK ISBN 9781852355661. £19.50; PBK. ISBN 978 1 85235 566 1 £12.00
Derek Mahon

In his *Essays in Appreciation*, Christopher Ricks considers the fate of Racine's *Phèdre* in English. As he points out, 'nothing of any lasting importance has ever been said about Racine in English' and 'no great writer in English has been profoundly fecundated by Racine'. Inspecting Robert Lowell's translation, he finds its showy flourishes 'appalling' and 'hideous', yet possessed of a 'corporeality' that 'transmits more of the energy of Racine, in a harshened form' than does Richard Wilbur's 'inoffensive' treatment of the play. While readers keen to add Derek Mahon's *Phaedra* to the mix will require his *Theatre* (also published by The Gallery Press) on top of the volume under review here, the polarity represented by those two American poets is everywhere on show in *Echo's Grove*. This is a book that features work 'after' a constellation of Greek, Latin, Chinese, Provençal, Irish, Italian, Norwegian, Spanish, Russian, German and Indian poets, but it is French-language poetry that has proved the most enduring of translator Mahon's muses. Most if not all his French versions, from the discarded attempt at Villon that concludes *Night-Crossing* (1968) to his recent adaptations of Michel Houellebecq, have been rhymed, and many incline towards the Wilbur end of the spectrum with a certain – conveniently French term – frou-frou quality. Here, for instance, is the Corbière of Mahon's 'Old Roscoff':

> Sleep in the dunes beneath the grey
> gunmetal clouds; the pennants gone,
> no grapeshot now will ricochet
> or drum rumble. Pungent dawn
> will find your children dream-ensnared
> by the great days when giants trod
> the timbered piers and cynosured
> the shopping lanes and promenade.

Mahon's poem is in four elegant seven-lines stanzas, but Corbière's original, picking its way through the crazy-paving of that poet's favoured ellipses, follows no such pattern. A practitioner of 'discordant, dislocated verse', in the words of the *Penguin Book of French Poetry*, Corbière did as much as anyone to wrench French poetry away from its incorrigibly decorative side.

'Cynosured' in the most elegantly gallic word in the above stanza, but has no basis in Corbière's original (*'Dors: sous les noires cheminées, /Écoute rêver tes enfants, /Mousses de quatre-vingts-dix ans, /Épaves des belles années...'*). (The two texts may have drifted well apart by now, but should 'shopping lanes' at the end of Mahon's stanza be 'shipping lanes'? Just a thought.)

It is not that Mahon cannot do slangy (cf. his *Cyrano de Bergerac*); the question is whether the element of 'consternation', to adapt Beckett on Kafka, is 'in the form' or 'behind the form'. Among the most revealing of Mahon's translations where all this is concerned is his wonderful version – surely one of the most accomplished translations in recent years – of Valéry's *Le cimetière marin*, 'The Seaside Cemetery'. There is something not just perfect but all-too-perfect about the poem, as it has already worked out for itself. There is the realisation of desiccation ('everything is exhausted, scorched by the air /into I don't know what rigorous form'), a yearning for the irrigation of the spoken word ('Where now are the colloquial turns of phrase'), the fear of over-ripeness and putrefaction ('But even as fruit consumes itself in taste, /even as it translates its own demise'), and finally the consciousness that the germ of change, error and decay amid so much Mediterranean stillness lies within the poet himself ('I am the one your worst fears validate – /my cowardice, my bad thoughts, my contrition /make up the one flaw in your precious opal').

Comparing the version printed here with Mahon's original text of 2001, I notice a sprinkling of revisions (no surprises there). What was once 'down the blue silence of celestial groves' in the first stanza has become 'down the blue calm of these celestial groves'. Both weigh in at eleven syllables, but the addition of 'these' tips the second decisively towards an English alexandrine, rendering more than a little otiose Mahon's insistence, in his foreword, on the skimpiness to a French ear of Valéry's ten-syllable French line. (Speaking of the foreword, I presume Mahon is being arch when he refers to this great masterpiece as a 'design classic' (!), a cheapening by association of the word 'classic' if ever there was one.) The stillness of Valéry's poem is a veneer, then, under which the poem is in fact a formicating mass of ambivalence, self-doubt and decay. As such, it forms an almost emblematic correlative for the arc of Mahon's career.

All of these larger questions aside, *Echo's Grove* is among the most bounteous and rewarding books of poetry of recent times. While the overlap with *Adaptations* (2006) is large, the new translations here from Ovid, Corbière, Laforgue and 'Gopal Singh', Mahon's sub-continental Katerina Brac, make this much more than an afterthought to the earlier volume. Among these 'sun-dazzled pages', where waves of translation break 'with ecstatic surges', Mahon provides as few others have done in contemporary times the 'shifting surface' where a truly polyglot poetry can flourish.

Aingeal Clare

*A Capital Union.* Saraband. ISBN 9781908643346. £8.99
Victoria Hendry

*A Capital Union* is a capital idea – in the current political climate, particularly. Victoria Hendry's first novel considers the response of some Scottish nationalists to wider international conflict during the Forties. Hendry sets the first and most significant sections of her story in Edinburgh during the Second World War, thereafter moving things to Ayrshire and Stirling in the later stages of the war and in the aftermath. This novel shows the terrible strain that ideological and military conflict can place on individuals beyond the battlefield itself.

Agnes is a young woman, recently married and living in Edinburgh's Morningside in the early years of the war. Brought up on a farm, Agnes gets by through growing vegetables in her back garden and setting a rabbit snare on the nearby Blackford Hill. She spends the rest of her time trying to be a supportive wife to her husband Jeff who works in the University on a Scots dictionary and is at the heart of the SNP during one of its most difficult periods. Her world is shaken by her husband's decision to sacrifice their personal happiness to his political beliefs. He refuses conscription, despite his own opposition to fascism and the difficulties Agnes faces in the enmity and anger of those among whom she must live her daily life. He elects to be sent to prison instead, as a 'Nationalist martyr'. This theme of the conflict between the political and the personal has echoes of Allan Massie, whose works are also often set in a world populated by those who can offer a pithy quotation from German or Greek literature over a whisky glass. Agnes doesn't have the education to understand all of these exchanges, though, and accordingly considers them a bit rude. She is an engaging narrator.

Hendry is also good at evoking the legendary stuffiness of some residents of Morningside and her recreations of wartime Edinburgh and the political meetings of the SNP in that period are entertaining. The Falkland Terrace of the novel is clearly Woodburn Terrace where it so happens I lived for a number of years, and the petty tyrannies of her neighbour Mrs MacDougall seem very familiar to me – as they probably will for many who have lived in a communal tenement stair. The way in which Agnes both goads and placates her neighbour is well drawn.

The police raid Agnes and Jeff's flat looking for compromising material on the SNP leadership. The presence of the police in turn frightens Mrs MacDougall into revealing to Agnes the occupant of the (supposedly empty) upstairs flat. There is a lovely Buchan-esque tinge to the discovery: the sense that international conflict is not something that is a distant concern, but rather something which is happening in the flat upstairs. Action and commitment are required from all of Buchan's characters and Hendry's Agnes is no different, but the boundaries of right and wrong have been redrawn since Buchan's jingoistic patriotism held sway, and Agnes' decision is far from simple. Her husband is brutalised by the strain of living up to his own patriotic idealism in such a hostile climate and she must look to others for some sort of salvation.

One of Buchan's talents is the skill with which he depicts his characters moving through a landscape but there is less of a sense of that, here. This seems something of a missed opportunity given the events which unfold. However, Hendry is perhaps writing to our own time in her skilful evocation of the significance of green places in the city itself.

> Some trees had tipped over in the gale but there was no one to clear them away. All the good, green places were going to sleep as if they had been enchanted, and the hard streets and barracks and docks were sucking all the men away...

This novel offers a real sense of the permanence and possibility of renewal offered by the natural world in the midst of conflict.

Hendry's use of the compilation of the Scots dictionary as a backdrop to her plot is interesting. Her husband, Jeff, had 'come to Ayrshire to collect words but collected me instead, saying it saved him searching all over the country when all the old words could be found right on the tip of my tongue.' Since she supposedly resembles Rita Hayworth, the idea of her being 'collected' by her husband is neatly put, and it is his attempt to define and control her that place a strain on their marriage. However, the Scots words – especially in the earlier stages of the novel – don't always seem to sit naturally on the tip of Agnes' tongue. Whether this is due to anxiety that a richer form of Scots wouldn't be understood by a wider audience or whether it's merely intended to represent the character herself attempting to conform linguistically to her new position as an 'Edinburgh lady', occasionally the Scots words seem to have landed by parachute in the midst of an otherwise convincing voice.

Victoria Hendry's novel is quickly engrossing and enjoyable. Ultimately, perhaps because the set up promises so much, the speed with which so many of the more rich elements and ideas of this novel are tied up or set to one side left me a little frustrated, because I wanted to remain in the midst of those tensions and complexities for a bit longer. *A Capital Union* offers an intriguing glimpse into the issues and characters of an earlier phase of the nationalist movement in Scotland. It is part of a re-examination of Scottish and British history as nationalism moves centre stage and it is an impressive debut.

Martin Philip

*A' Bhàrdachd Ghàidhlig* (edited by Moray Watson). Acair..ISBN 9780861523139. £15
Iain Mac a' Ghobhainn

Iain Crichton Smith (1928–98) was a notably prolific writer and his output included a considerable body of poems in Gaelic. These have now been collected in an almost exhaustive monolingual edition with a serviceable introduction and notes by Moray Watson of Aberdeen University.

Posthumous editions of this nature can sometimes diminish a poet's status by the inclusion of inferior material against the author's wishes. This welcome collection tends not to, I think, by virtue of the consistent voice over the course of fifty years in Smith's poetry. There is a fuguistic element to it in that certain images – nylon, neon, shadows, letters, crayons, orchestras – are invoked again and again. Smith's thematic range is not extensive but his treatment of it is. His poetry is discursive, lyrical, elegiac, elliptical, epigrammatic, surrealistic, abstract, occasionally imagistic and rarely didactic. His best work of this type to my mind is the late sequence *Na h-Eilthirich/ The Exiles* in which many of the elements of his poetic apparatus in Gaelic synthesise and resonate.

In a poem from the late sequence 'An t-Eilean'/'The Island', Smith wrote: 'I was between the songs of William Ross and the poems of Milton, "the keys lost and blind looking for them"./One language is a perfume, the other is in my brain'. In 'My Typewriter' he has: My typewriter on the table, / my slave and my master. / One alphabet will do / for English and Gaelic. / Those stars are black / and the sky behind them yellow. / I'm sitting/between two worlds / with my kind keys." In line with this, there are Gaelic poems here which are represented, if not actually directly translated, in English (such as 'An Dèidh Blàr Chùil Lodair'/'Culloden and After').

Notably absent, as the editor acknowledges, are Smith's Gaelic versions of Catullus, Lowell, Carlos Williams, Auden, Larkin, Quasimodo *et al.*, which I would consider at least as informative in terms of the poet's development as other elements mentioned in the introduction and notes. Nor have his sensitive and humorous verses for children been included.

In terms of simple explication, Dr Watson's commentary can hardly be faulted. The notes accompanying each poem start with a line-count. The critical attitude is descriptive and, as such, of a piece with the great bulk of discursive writing in Gaelic and at variance with, as an isolated example, the more rigorous associative work of Peter Mackay. It is not entirely clear who the commentary is intended for but Watson describes his editing as 'light'. The critical lexicon employed abounds in neutral epithets – renowned, skilful, strong, clear, exceptional, effective and so on. Would that count for much as criticism in English?

Occasionally Dr Watson mixes his metaphors with his metonyms (he doesn't use the word metonymy or its Gaelic equivalent). Time and again he explains how a certain poem 'shows the great interest the poet had' in, for example (another of his favourite usages): death, 'knowledge, insight and understanding', 'the way in which time goes by and how age descends on people and the effect time has on people (particularly in relation to the memory of youth, beauty and ability)', 'age and what it would be like to be quite old knowing that death must be near', Napoleon ('such a talented chancellor') and so on. He goes on: 'time and age are important themes', 'humour was just as important to Smith as the serious themes people write about' and 'spring symbolises renewal. But there's no renewal for those that are dead'. The poem 'Air Latha Brèagha' is described as 'a series of images about a good day' and poem no. 256 in the sequence is about Elvis 'dying after ruining his health by eating too much'. Then there's a note on Wittgenstein who 'did important work' and another that *whatstheworldcomingto?* is 'quite a common complaint'. There's rather a bit too much about the primary environment and mirrors, not to mention *Dallas* ('an American programme which millions of people used to watch in many countries in the 1980s. It is used here as a metonym for the American cultural empire which is growing everywhere.')

This collection, however, confirms Iain Crichton Smith's reputation as one of the most important of all Gaelic poets and Dr Watson has done a great service for Gaelic literature as textual editor if rather less as commentator.

Rody Gorman

# Notes on Contributors

Fran Brearton is Professor of Modern Poetry at Queen's University Belfast. She co-edited (with Alan Gillis) *The Oxford Handbook of Modern Irish Poetry* (2012), and has recently edited a new edition of Robert Graves's *Good-bye to All That* for Penguin Classics (forthcoming, 2014).

Colette Bryce's books include *The Full Indian Rope Trick* and *Self-Portrait in the Dark* (both Picador). A new collection is forthcoming in September. She received the Cholmondeley Award for her poetry in 2010.

Ciaran Carson was born in 1948 in Belfast. He is the author of a body of work which includes poetry, prose and translation. His *Collected Poems* was published in 2008 and a novel, *The Pen Friend*, in 2009. He is Professor of Poetry at Queen's University Belfast. His most recent book is *In the Light Of*, adaptations from Rimbaud's *Illuminations*.

Regi Claire was born and brought up in Switzerland. She has twice been shortlisted for a Saltire Book of the Year Award. One of her stories was selected for *The Best British Short Stories 2013* (Salt). She is a Royal Literary Fund Fellow.

Aingeal Clare has written for *The Guardian*, the *London Review of Books*, and the *TLS*. She lives in Aberdeenshire.

Miriam Gamble is a poet and critic from Belfast. Her first collection, *The Squirrels are Dead*, was published by Bloodaxe in 2010 and won a Somerset Maugham award in 2011; her second, *Pirate Music*, is forthcoming in September 2014. She teaches Creative Writing at the University of Edinburgh.

Rody Gorman, born in Dublin in 1960, lives on Skye. His most recent collection is *Beartan Briste*, 2011. He edits the annual Scottish and Irish Gaelic anthology *An Guth*.

Colin Graham's most recent book is *Northern Ireland: 30 Years of Photography*. Other books include *Deconstructing Ireland* and *Ideologies of Epic*. He writes for *The Dublin Review*, *Source* and *The Vacuum* and is co-editor of *The Irish Review*.

Brian Hamill lives in Glasgow. Brian has been writing since he first attended creative writing classes at Glasgow University in 2007. He won the Scottish Book Trust New Writers Award 2012, and is Submissions Editor for *thi wurd* fiction magazine.

David Harsent's *Legion*, won the Forward Prize for best collection 2005; *Night* (2011) won the Griffin International Poetry Prize. *In Secret*, his English versions of poems by Yannis Ritsos, was published in 2012. A new collection, *Standing Shadows*, will appear later this year. Harsent has collaborated with composers – most often with

Harrison Birtwistle – on commissions that have been performed world wide. He is Professor of Creative Writing at the University of Roehampton.

W.N. Herbert is Professor of Poetry and Creative Writing at Newcastle University. Recent work includes, with Yang Lian, *Jade Ladder* (2012), an anthology of contemporary Chinese poetry, and *The Third Shore* (2013), translations between English-speaking and Chinese poets; with Andy Jackson, *Whaleback City* (2013), an anthology of Dundee poetry. His own poetry includes *Omnesia*, and *Murder Bear* (both 2013).

Maria Johnston frequently contributes essays on and reviews of contemporary poetry to journals such as *Poetry Ireland Review* and *Tower Poetry* and is the co-editor (with Philip Coleman) of *Reading Pearse Hutchinson: 'From Findrum to Fisterra'* (Irish Academic Press, 2011).

Paul Maddern gained his PhD from Queen's University Belfast and is Teaching Fellow in Creative Writing at the University of Leeds. The Beachcomber's Report (Templar: 2010) was shortlisted for the Eithne Strong Award and won the Bermuda Government Literary Prize for Poetry.

Simon Malpas teaches English Literature at Edinburgh University. His most recent book, co-written with Andrew Taylor and published by Manchester University Press, is on Thomas Pynchon.

Peter McDonald's *Collected Poems* was published by Carcanet in 2012. He is Christopher Tower Student and Tutor in Poetry in the English Language at Christ Church, Oxford.

Jane McKie's books and pamphlets include *Morocco Rococo* (Cinnamon Press), which was awarded the 2008 Sundial/Scottish Arts Council prize for best first book of 2007, *When the Sun Turns Green* (Polygon, 2009) and *Garden of Bedsteads* (Mariscat, 2011). She won the 2011 Edwin Morgan International Poetry Competition and currently teaches at the University of Edinburgh.

Dennis O'Driscoll (1954–2012) wrote eight books of poetry, all published by The Gallery Press, including *New and Selected Poems* (2004), a Poetry Book Society Special Commendation, *Reality Check* (2007) and *Dear Life* (Winner of the Irish Times Poetry Now Award, 2012). His essays and reviews have appeared widely, and *Stepping Stones: Interviews with Seamus Heaney* (2008), was shortlisted for 'Book of the Decade' in the Irish Book Awards 2010. He died on Christmas Eve 2012.

Ricardo Pau-Llosa has published seven books of poetry, the last five with Carnegie Mellon University Press in Pittsburgh, Pennsylvania (USA). His work has appeared in *American Poetry Review*, *Ambit*, *The Fiddlehead*, *Kenyon Review*, *Ploughshares*, *PN Review*, *Poetry*, *Stand*, *Southern Review*, *Vallum*, among many other journals. He is also a widely published art critic. More at www.pau-llosa.com.

Martin Philip is a lecturer, writer and musician. He has taught literature and creative writing with the Open University for a number of years and teaches part-time at the University of Edinburgh whilst completing his second novel.

Simon Pomery lives in London. His recent work has been published by *Edinburgh Review*, the *Times Literary Supplement*, and *The White Review*. A new pamphlet of work, *Defence Against a Knife Attack*, is due in 2014.

Dilys Rose lives in Edinburgh. She has published ten books, including *Pest Maiden*, *Lord of Illusions* and *Bodywork* and also enjoys creative collaborations with visual artists and composers. Her new novel, *Pelmanism*, is forthcoming from Luath Press this summer.

Daniel Shand is a PhD student at the University of Edinburgh. In 2012 he won the Sloan Prize for short fiction in Scots and has performed his work at the Edinburgh Book Festival. He is currently working on something longer.

Allyson Stack's fiction has appeared in numerous publications and she is currently writing a novel-in-stories, *Motherland*. A lecturer in Literature and Creative Writing at the University of Edinburgh, she is working on a scholarly monograph, *Edith Wharton and the Question of Criticism*; her article on the work of Jean Laplanche will be reprinted in *Seductions and Enigmas: Cultural Readings with Laplanche* (Lawrence & Wishart, 2014).

David Wheatley is the author of four poetry collections with The Gallery Press, most recently *A Nest on the Waves,* and edited Samuel Beckett's *Selected Poems 1930–1989* for Faber. He lives in Aberdeenshire.

Ben Wilkinson is a literary critic and writes regularly for the *Guardian* and the *TLS*. He works as an editor for the Poetry Archive, and is completing research in contemporary poetry at Sheffield Hallam University. His own poetry has been shortlisted for numerous awards including the inaugural Picador Poetry Prize. He is working towards a first full collection.

# How to Subscribe to Edinburgh Review

Individual subscriptions (3 issues annually) £20 within the UK; £28 abroad.

Institutional subscriptions (3 issues annually) £35 within the UK; £43 abroad.

You can subscribe online at www.edinburgh-review.com
or send a cheque to

Edinburgh Review
22a Buccleuch Place
Edinburgh EH8 9LN

Most back issues are available at £7.99 each.

You'll find the new *Edinburgh Review* website at

# http://www.edinburgh-review.com

Please join us on Facebook and Twitter.